ADVANCE PRAISE FOR

A SOUL-CENTERED APPROACH TO EDUCATING TEACHERS: A BLACK EDUCATION NETWORK (ABEN)

"Most people would agree that these are troubling times for Black people worldwide. Fortunately, *A Soul-Centered Approach to Educating Teachers: A Black Education Network (ABEN)* provides our communities a framework and praxis for those who educate across geographical and cultural locations. This book, steeped in the Pan-African and Black liberation tradition, introduces spirituality, culture, and healing into our daily ponderings and practices of education reform. The editors brought together some of the most prolific thinkers interested in education for liberation. They've made the case that ABEN is a hidden gem in liberation work!"

Venus E. Evans-Winters, Professor,
Founder of Planet Venus Institute

"The work of ABEN and its founder, Mama Debra Watkins, is sacred work in the best tradition of the Ancestors. This volume is a much-needed and necessary documentation of insights, methods and outcomes that bear witness to effective African-centered leadership, instruction, engagement and achievement."

Chike Akua, Ph.D.,
Assistant Professor of Educational Leadership,
Clark Atlanta University

"Simply put, re-building the Black Teacher Pipeline necessitates revitalizing the soul of Black teachers. In *A Soul-Centered Approach to Educating Teachers: A Black Education Network (ABEN)*, we receive an effective blueprint to unite Black teachers, but we are also reminded of how critical Afro-centrism is to pedagogy, generational knowledge, and our pursuit of justice.

The best teachers of my life were situated at Nidhamu Sasa and they embodied their souls in their collective practices. Their influence has impressed upon me that to rebuild the Black Teacher Pipeline, we must prioritize fueling the soul of Black teachers and paving the way to allow them to integrate themselves in impactful Black teacher pedagogies and Black historical lenses. The triumph of *A Soul-Centered Approach to Educating Teachers: A Black Education Network (ABEN)* is demonstrating how impactful this vision is when fully realized and giving a powerful example for us all to model. I'm humbled to be a part of this movement towards "retrieving our . . . human heart."

S. El-Mekki, CEO,
Center for Black Educator Development

A SOUL-CENTERED APPROACH TO EDUCATING TEACHERS

A SOUL-CENTERED APPROACH TO EDUCATING TEACHERS

A Black Education Network (ABEN)

EDITED BY RONA M. FREDERICK

AND KMT SHOCKLEY

Myers Education Press

Gorham, Maine

Myers Education Press

Published by Myers Education Press, LLC
P.O. Box 424
Gorham, ME 04038

Myers Education Press is an academic publisher specializing in books, e-books and digital content in the field of education. All of our books are subjected to a rigorous peer review process and produced in compliance with the standards of the Council on Library and Information Resources.

Library of Congress Cataloging-in-Publication Data available from Library of Congress.

13-digit ISBN 978-1-9755-0569-1 (paperback)
13-digit ISBN 978-1-9755-0570-7 (library networkable e-edition)
13-digit ISBN 978-1-9755-0571-4 (consumer e-edition)

Printed in the United States of America.

All first editions printed on acid-free paper that meets the American National Standards Institute Z39-48 standard.

Books published by Myers Education Press may be purchased at special quantity discount rates for groups, workshops, training organizations and classroom usage. Please call our customer service department at 1-800-232-0223 for details.

Cover design by Benita Lovett-Rivera.

Visit us on the web at **www.myersedpress.com** to browse our complete list of titles.

Contents

FOREWORD

“Ubuntu! Who We Are and Why”

Joyce E. King, PhD

> It may look as if all we ever did was to endure this history of ruin, taking no steps to end the negative slide and begin the positive turn. That impression is false. Over the disastrous millennia there have been Africans concerned to work out solutions to our problems and to act on them.
>
> —*Ayi Kwei Armah, Osiris Rising, p. 9*

IT HAS BEEN MY HONOR and privilege to witness, support, and benefit professionally and personally from Debra Watkins' visionary leadership of A'BEN's[1] community networking programs and partnerships, which this timely book documents so powerfully. Apt metaphors for A'BEN might be: It's like dropping a pebble in a pond as the implications and far-reaching influences reverberate. Or A'BEN grows and nourishes new capacities in people like a rhizome—an underground stem system with the healing properties of a plant like ginger. A'BEN is rooted in Black knowledge, traditions, and values. In this book, Debra and the coeditors, Rona Frederick and Kmt Shockley, lift up and celebrate the generative power of Black educational excellence that A'BEN has been quietly making possible for students, families, and educators across the nation and beyond for decades. A'BEN's unique, historically significant story merits the scholarly examination presented in this book and much broader public recognition is overdue.

Although we typically understand networking as “exchanging information,” “making connections,” and “building relationships,” A Black Education Network (A'BEN) has demonstrated truly emancipatory collaborations that have involved so much more. I recall visiting Debra's office once and talking with her about the way she was engaging and educating parents whose children were participating in the Greene Scholars STEM program. I was present at a Greene Scholars Science Fair at a time when there was little attention in the academic community focused on Black children and science. This holistic community-centered approach that was clearly missing in educational practice has been part and parcel of A'BEN's innovative power to transform the lives of students as well as our own imaginations as educators.

Perhaps several other examples will suffice. Nearly 10 years ago, a group of us working with Debra called 45 other seasoned educators and activists from Black communities across the nation to Atlanta to plan a National Black Education Summit. We dubbed this convening "the Atlanta 45." Imagine a convening that includes scholars, elders, pastors, parents, community activists all in the same space with one mindset. During that 2-day working meeting, we met dynamic leaders such as Fluke Fluker, the former Marine, high school teacher, education activist, and cofounder and president of The Village Nation in Los Angeles. Fluke reminded us that when the Masai people greet each other, they ask: "And how are the children?" When our conversations faltered around political disagreements—charter school folks versus anticharter school folk, Dr. Elaine Mosely cut to the chase saying: "We ought to be about educating our children wherever they are." Our Queen Mother of Black Education, Dr. Adelaide Sanford, offered her inimitable wisdom as well, reminding us that we are "beloved." Dr. Iva Carruthers' incomparable organizing experience moved our agenda forward to Chicago, where she was one of the anchors for the Chicago Summit, which drew participants from as far away as the historic Black communities in Nova Scotia. Some of my doctoral students who participated in the Summit were never the same after that experience. A'BEN has grown and developed out of this kind of victorious collective consciousness.

During the Atlanta 45 convening, Debra announced her intention to organize support for 1,000 African-centered schools. This was an incredibly bold vision that reverberated throughout and energized the Chicago Summit. Although her support of a specific number of schools remains an inspiring goal, what is more significant are the rhizomic above and below ground connections that Debra establishes serving educators, institutions, and grassroots organizations and bringing them together across the education spectrum. Through such relationships in courageous defense of Black children, A'BEN has evolved into strategic partnering approaches toward Black education for liberation. And we know that Black liberation is the pathway to human freedom for everyone. In fact, when we convened a second grand gathering in Chicago, The Black Education Congress the following year, we further cemented the knowledge sharing that continues to elevate the work of A'BEN.

As a member of A'BEN's wisdom circle, one of my contributions was to help name the new organization that Debra envisioned. We decided that "a ben," the Songhoy phrase that essentially means "the buck stops here," would advance our connection with our African heritage in meaningful ways. African language concepts are a much-needed Black liberation dynamic. Likewise, A'BEN's logo that incorporates the Akan Adinkra Sankofa symbol, "Go back, fetch, and act," conveys the Pan-African ethos. It is also worth noting that rather than regaling the accomplishments of a single individual in Eurocentric fashion—notwithstanding Debra Watkins' undeniably impressive contributions—and in keeping with an African-centered "Ubuntu–I am because we are" approach, this book centers and celebrates the authentic voices of others whom Debra and A'BEN have inspired. It is collective work and responsibility that has made A'BEN's nourishing, knowledge-building networking possible, scalable, and replicable—networking in the Black teaching/organizing for communal excellence tradition that effectively disrupts historical patterns of Black educational disenfranchisement.

I chose to begin this Foreword with the epigraph above because it beautifully describes what A'BEN does "to end the negative slide." This book demonstrates what happens when visionary, dedicated educators, and community activists guided by our tradition of academic and cultural excellence come together using both financial and cultural resources to mobilize relationships to "work out solutions to our problems and to act on them." Asa Hilliard, Barbara Sizemore, Donald Smith—renowned educators who are all ancestors now—helped us understand that Black children need education and socialization for both academic and cultural excellence or ACE, a foundation element of A'BEN's mission and practice. As Gloria Ladson-Billings (1994) explains, ACE means preparing our children to "hold their own in the classroom" and not "forget about their own in the community."

The multiple, intergenerational voices in this book delineate A'BEN's evidence-based beneficial impacts in numerous educational settings and community contexts, from the prescience of the Greene Scholars STEM program, 17 years of culturally responsive professional development provided to school leaders, teachers, and teacher educators at the popular Stanford Summer Institutes, to the Cultural Imperative Initiative that Tony Browder has offered in schools with A'BEN support, an initiative that is critically needed given current efforts to censor the curriculum. A'BEN has also catalyzed the development of a statewide Black Student Union movement and a Cultural Ambassadors program for college and university students. Each of these signature A'BEN initiatives is a potential multiplier, enabling participants to impact education in ways beyond their direct engagement with A'BEN activities.

I also chose the epigraph above because the novel, *Osiris Rising*, written by the prodigious Ghanaian author, Ayi Kwei Armah, illustrates some of the interconnecting relationships with Black education innovation and leadership that Debra and I have experienced. Twenty years ago, Baba Asa Hilliard, Nana Baffour Amankwatia II, gave me Armah's book to inform my work as chair of the American Educational Research Association's Commission on Research in Black Education (CORIBE). Dr. Asa G. Hilliard served on the CORIBE Elders Council. This research and action initiative served as a hub for other significant relationship building. Susan Taylor, former editor of *Essence Magazine*, was an avid and engaged CORIBE Commissioner. Susan let me know that Debra Watkins was doing amazing work in California that aligned with the Commission's goals and suggested that I contact her. Although Susan was based in New York City, through her network, she had learned about Debra Watkins and the California Alliance of African American Educators (CAAAE, the forerunner of A'BEN).

I reached out to Debra, and she reminded me that we already knew each other. Indeed, Debra recalled that when she was teaching English at Independence High School in San Jose, California, and I was a professor and director of Teacher Education at Santa Clara University, she had invited me to participate in a program that she organized at the high school. Our collaborations have continued to prosper. Although Debra likes to "blame" me for urging her to expand her educational initiatives to serve a national constituency, she was already developing a national reputation! By generously sharing her relationships and her fund-raising expertise, Debra's leadership of A'BEN has connected an impressive and influential network of education experts, theorists, practitioners, and rights holders (not stakeholders, as our friend, graphic designer Benita Lovett-Rivera, reminds us), who have been engaged with and supported by A'BEN's stellar programs.

Returning to Ayi Kwei Armah's divinatory message, I conclude with another excerpt from *Osiris Rising* as a Coda to emphasize what I believe reflects A'BEN's ethical significance as a model empowering social change strategy for liberating Black education. Amidst distressingly low levels of educational attainment for too many of our children, the violence of rampaging curriculum censorship, and other forms of immoral deadly violence being perpetuated against our people with impunity, A'BEN stands in the breach, showing us a spiritually informed way forward that is solidly rooted in our cultural heritage of collective resistance. Thus, let us all say emphatically and unapologetically:

> We are not after the slave-foreman power that, under the killer's continuing rule, is blind ambition's hollow prize. We are after intelligent understanding of all our realities, not simply the politics of power. We are after intelligent action to change these realities. For we intend, as Africans, to retrieve our human face, our human heart, the human mind our ancestors taught to soar. That is who we are, and why (Armah, 1995, p. 10).

Note

1. This spelling of A'BEN honors its link to the Songhoy language. However, it is commonly spelled ABEN and used in that manner throughout the rest of this book.

References

Armah, A. K. (1995). *Osiris rising: A novel of African past, present and future.* Per Ankh Press.

Ladson-Billing, G. (1994). *The dreamkeepers: Successful teachers of African American children* (2nd ed.). Jossey-Bass.

Founder's Introduction

Debra Watkins

It is easier to build strong children than to repair broken men

—*Frederick Douglass*

WHEN I FIRST ENVISIONED WHAT this book would entail, I was excited about its chronicling the 20 impactful years of A Black Education Network (formerly called the California Alliance of African American Educators, CAAAE) with an emphasis on the highly acclaimed Summer Institutes we started in 2002 focused on Pedagogies and Practices for Successfully Reaching African American Students. The Institutes, created with Dr. Linda Darling Hammond, a professor at Stanford University's School of Education, intentionally elevated Black scholarship and featured world-renowned educators.

After I selected Dr. Rona Frederick to serve as the primary editor, all of that changed! In her wisdom, she saw a much more expansive story that went well beyond the Summer Institutes to focus on the great work we did "outside the White gaze," to quote the brilliant Toni Morrison.

The pivot was not challenging because I already had in mind some of the people who would help tell the story of ABEN's sustaining success:

- Mark and Mahea Gaskins had attended the Institutes for several years and ABEN helped inspire them to create The Village Method;
- Mama Rosaline Preudhomme came into my life just a few years ago, but her impact on my spiritual grounding has been immeasurable;
- Bobbie Brooks had served as the founder of CAAAE's only chapter and grew it significantly over a 9-year period as leader before passing it on to one of her board members (Dr. Robyn Fisher) who used it as the springboard to establish the highly effective African American Regional Educational Alliances (AAREA);
- Anthony Browder became my business partner after he keynoted a national conference in Chicago in 2013, underwritten primarily by the CAAAE, that served as the catalyst for the creation of what would become ABEN;

- Akosua Lesesne was present at ABEN's regional conference in Philadelphia and asked me to be her jegna;
- Monica Utsey, cofounder of Sankofa Homeschool Collective, was instrumental in helping ABEN support Black families who suddenly found themselves homeschooling during the Pandemic and she also helped coordinate our virtual tours to Ghana;
- Ayinde Olukoton was an outstanding student in the Dr. Frank S. Greene Scholars Program focused on STEM that I created in 2001 and a youth civic ambassador for justice, so he was well-equipped to offer a youth perspective.

I knew it was important for my jegna, the brilliant Dr. Joyce King, to weigh in on the project because she has been the wind beneath my wings since I first started the CAAAE in 2001. Dr. Rona (Frederick) brought Marvin Lynn's acumen to the project and he has done an outstanding job of synthesizing ABEN's work.

While working on my chapter, I was half-way through Dr. Jarvis Givens' (2021) *Fugitive Pedagogy: Carter G. Woodson and the Art of Black Teaching* when it dawned on me that his characterization of Dr. Woodson's work was an apt description of how I led the work described in this book. Since 2001, I have raised millions of dollars for three institutions that I have founded or cofounded: ABEN, Black Students of California United (BSCU), and the Dr. Frank S. Greene Scholars Program. Like Dr. Woodson, I committed my life to creating and sustaining Black institutions while maintaining a consistent suspicion of White paternalism. Even as I provide capacity-building for Black-led organizations, I do so with the understanding that their missions will not be coopted either. They will continue to offer programs that are liberatory and unfettered by what White people think is best for Black people.

Dr. Woodson insisted on pursuing White philanthropic dollars and access to opportunities for expanding the work of the Association for the Study of Negro Life and History (ASNLH) even as he refused White control over its agenda. As you read this book, be very clear that all of the work described was done without one White person directing it.

In fact, when it comes to the Summer Institutes, I intentionally chose to feature only Black scholars because academia is racist and their work is often denigrated or ignored there. I have heard from several Black scholars about how they were denied tenure or access to research funding because White people did not believe that their focus on Black life was "rigorous" enough. Like Dr. Woodson, I am committed to the idea that philanthropists should not dictate the research agenda of Black scholars and their intellectual work.

As Rona, Kmt, and I were bringing this book to a close, something magical happened. When I first started teaching in 1977, I channeled those educators who had poured into me as I matriculated from grades K-12. They saw my humanity, embraced my potential, and nurtured it. When Tricia M. Kress, Christopher Emdin, and Robert Lake published the book entitled *Critical Pedagogy For Healing: Paths Beyond "Wellness," Toward A Soul Revival of Teaching and Learning* (2022), I knew that I had finally found the word that defines my vision for 1,000 schools—soul-centered. There is a place for spirituality, faith, and hope; physical and mental well-being; arts and creativity; community and connection; and space, place, and land.

I started incubating A Black Education Network (ABEN) in 2012 after what was then called the California Alliance of African American Educators (CAAAE) had helped convene close to 200 "conscious" Black educators and community activists from around the country for a two-day conference at the Westin O'Hare in Chicago. My vision was for a network of 1,000 schools where all of the Black children were achieving at grade level or above and where they were joyful learners. That place is soul-centered. It is a place where everyone on the campus has committed to not inflicting harm. Instead of curricular trauma, there is culturally relevant curriculum. Students are seen and loved and they know it. They look forward to attending school.

When I first consulted Dr. King about what to even call the new national organization that I was building, she emphasized how important it was for "network" to be a part of the name. Dr. King believes in the "big tent" approach where every member of the Black community is valuable regardless of educational achievement or economic status. I wholeheartedly agree. It was also important to Dr. King that we use the word Black. In the Songhoy language, Black only has positive connotations unlike the negative ones in English that we are bombarded with from birth. Of course, we had to spell out that we were focused on education. When we came up with A Black Education Network, Dr. Hassimi Maiga, a brilliant Songhoy chief and professor, pointed out that A'BEN means "the buck stops here" or "it is finished" in his language. I was thrilled with that acronym because I have always felt that

WE are the ones who ultimately should craft, execute, and sustain liberatory education for Black people.

Building ABEN was not without its challenges and I learned a lot of lessons along the way. People often asked me to write a book about how I built institutions that are still thriving so I published *Thoughts Held Hostage: A Black Teacher's Journey of Unlocking Young Minds* in 2016. Here are the lessons learned from the final chapter in that book:

1. Thank people.
2. Affirm people.
3. Listen to people.
4. Believe in people.
5. Build alliances.
6. Show results.
7. Think big.
8. Follow your passion.
9. Strive for excellence.
10. Work hard and smart.

As you engage with this book, please recognize that all of our lives are interconnected in some way by virtue of the fact that we reside on this fragile planet called Earth. We breathe the same air and the world rotates on its axis for each of us in the same manner. I thank God and the ancestors for placing in me a desire and the skills to create and sustain institutions that have already positively impacted thousands of lives and will continue to do so for decades to come.

I am especially grateful to my mother, Rosie Mae Masters, for instilling in me a love of people and a commitment to lift as I climb.

"To leave the door open and the ladder down" is a motto that my dear friend and ABEN's first board chair, Bernard Kinsey, has used to order his steps in life. I embrace it wholeheartedly and add my own adage "to whom much is given, much is required."

The journey has been an honor.

Editors' Introduction

Rona M. Frederick, PhD and Kmt Shockley, PhD

Introduction

Debra Watkins defines a soul-centered approach to education as one in which the teacher sees the "soul" or humanity of him/herself and its connection to the "soul" or humanity of the students in his/her classroom. As a result, the teacher prepares lessons and connects with the student in ways that honor the dignity, experiences, history, and, most importantly, ways of knowing. This way of thinking also honors the spirit of both the cared for and the caregiver. It works in direct opposition to the objectification of Black teachers, researchers, and academicians who are often ignored in reform policy focused on improving US education. Watkins understands that educating Black children is not a race conversation in the language of "gaps" and "opportunities," juxtaposing Whiteness and Blackness, but a question of culture—a culture which in turns connects us to what Egun Kwame Agyei Akoto and Akua Akoto call the "Sankofa movement," which refers to our destiny to return, retrieve, and restore that which was lost during the *maafa* (period of enslavement and great destruction). Debra Watkins asks, "What are the ways that communities of African ancestry come together to define and deliver best practices based on history, commonalities and themes that make sense for Black children?"

Stories of Black children being dehumanized while matriculating through the U.S. system are far too common and beg the question for those in academia, school settings, and other teacher training programs: How do we serve Black children in ways that truly nourish their souls? In the U.S. context, communities of African ancestry in the United States are often taught by those who don't know our story—our experiences, our culture, our ways of knowing—and there are few outlets in academia to foster those spaces and collaboration in so-called teacher education programs, alternative certification, conferences, or otherwise.

In 1903, Du Bois prophetically argued the idea that although Black folks are faced with the horrific everyday reality of systemic racism and dehumanizing macro and microaggressions, somehow our souls remain intact, ready and willing to fight and possibly triumph. Despite decades of terror, pieces of our soul hold onto our genetic memory and our fire to be free. Debra Watkins' goal, in the words of Asa Hilliard, is to reawaken the African mind and reorientate teachers, children, and the larger community.

As Kmt Shockley and I discussed the work of A Black Education Network (ABEN), we were most drawn to its creation of a sacred space that begins and ends with African ways of knowing. The term *African* in this case includes communities of African ancestry located throughout the diaspora. Unlike traditional teacher education programs that are grounded in White ideology, hierarchy, and anti-Black practices, ABEN understands that Black scholarship is held by the community, not only in academia. It is inclusive of academia but expansive in that it acknowledges and embraces the voices of practitioners, administrators, parents, etc. and their expertise in educating Black youth. Debra Watkins convenes networks of Black educators who deeply understand the indigenous connections from past to present while simultaneously looking forward. Without creating Blackness as a monolith, she pulls from African-centered practices that make sense for Black youth.

As a leader, Debra Watkins also recognizes the importance of being flexible when the situation requires. The way ABEN adjusted and shifted in the context of the Pandemic, immediately pivoting to online classes and virtual trips to Ghana to support the education of Black youth, is an example of her flexibility. Offering master classes in culturally responsive teaching and African-centered thought and theory to young people who had never experienced a Black teacher is yet another example. The benefit was undeniable, not only for students but also for grassroots organizers who have now expanded their reach and practice.

A major goal of this book project is to demonstrate the impact and benefits of ABEN and its programming. ABEN allows community members to systematically access African ways of knowing and being and allows those who are unfamiliar to come into their Africaness or expand their resources or support systems to center the experiences of African people in their work in educating children. ABEN systemized African thought in practice in their Cultural Imperative Program designed by Anthony Browder, and in the Greene Scholars Science Program.

Another goal is to chronicle the steps of a forward-thinking leader. From teacher activist to community organizer and philanthropist, Debra Watkins mastered how to engage an audience as the context changes. Her flexibility in content delivery allows her to pivot. For example, the Summer Institute held on the Stanford University campus worked well until the Pandemic determined otherwise. Thus, the Institute went virtual, extending to the homeschooling community and expanding ABEN's programming without missing a step, developing intercontinental content well suited for African children across the diaspora. Webinars and podcasts also enabled Debra Watkins to have a wider reach.

A final goal of this project is to offer a blueprint for building an organization. Nuanced in the writing are ways that Debra Watkins networked, organized, and built a sustainable program. The reader will learn about organizations she joined, conversations she had to solicit funds, as well as how she built a solid team of philanthropic supporters.

This book is a combination of oral narratives and first-person storytelling about ABEN's impact on communities in the United States and abroad. We embraced all of the participants' storytelling styles and believe that they each added a 360-degree view to the work of ABEN over time. We also explored the nuances of programming, networking, and leadership as both a blueprint and a methodology toward best practice for both community organizing and the development of a sustainable network of Black excellence. We added action-oriented questions at the end of each chapter as a nod to the work done at the Summer Institutes as there is always praxis where there is ABEN. Finally, in the framing of this book, we pay homage to leaders that influenced Black education and the work of ABEN, in turn, providing ways for the reader to revisit the work of great pioneers of Black education across the African diaspora.

For a year, I (Rona Frederick) sat with Debra Watkins once a week for about an hour via ZOOM, interviewing her about her life history, practice, experience, and perceptions. QSR International's NVIVO qualitative software was used to analyze the oral narratives, which were then coded and themed based on African-centered and culturally responsive literature, paying close attention to the voice of the participant. In order to capture a 360-degree view of ABEN, we encouraged the voices of all kinds of educators to share their experiences of ABEN. This volume includes a chapter on those who do grassroots organizing such as Monica Utsey, cofounder of the Sankofa Homeschool Collective; Mahea and Mark Gaskins, founders of the Village Method; brother Ayinde, who was a very successful Greene Scholar student. Debra Watkins' jegna, Dr. Joyce King, who served as an intellectual support and guide; and Egyptologist Anthony T. Browder, who designed the Cultural Imperative Program. In some cases, participants were interviewed and in other cases, narratives are written in first person. Whether colloquial or academic, in all cases we honored the stories told and we learned from the change makers that compose ABEN.

Readers of this volume will find that Debra Watkins responds to Egun Asa Hilliard's imposing question, "Do we have the will to educate all children?" with a resounding *yes*! ABEN not only has the will, but also the track record demonstrating that when our culture is used as a guide, not only can we educate all children, we can use that culture as a guide to restore humanity to the world. In that sense, the work of ABEN and the power of African-Centered Education (ACE) are not just guideposts for Black education but also guideposts that the field of education itself should be using to envisage positive change in the failing system of public education in the United States. This volume witnesses how the vision of Debra Watkins, the institutionalization of ABEN, and the power and prowess of ACE combine to create a living model for the rejuvenation of Black education and African indigeneity. The *nyansa nananom* (order of our ancestors), their wisdom and guidance, and their teachings are the fuel of this work. In that sense, not only do we have a response to Egun Asa Hilliard's critical question, ABEN is also providing the prescriptions that are evident within the corpus of the *nyansa nananom* from time immemorial.

The prescriptions include, as our ancestors would say, "eating" *Maat*—that is, consuming truth, justice, harmony, reciprocity, balance, order, and propriety as a way of life so much so that *Maat* becomes part of the DNA. *Maat* becomes the raison d'être of this work. The work exists not just to illuminate the model, but also to connect to and become part of the intergenerational cultural transmission process. In the aforementioned senses, the chapters should be read as responses to ancestral calls to restore *Maat* and engage in Sankofa for the purpose of providing another link in the chain toward the revivification and reclamation of African sovereignty utilizing the vehicle of what, in this moment, we call education.

This work is a long time coming. One teacher with a big dream—ABEN—1,000 Black schools. To this we say—*Ashe!*

Terms

African-centered education (ACE) is rooted in the unique history of the evolved culture of African people. It is defined by its singular commitment to the elucidation of that history, that culture, and the confirmation, invigoration, and perpetuation of the African collective identity that emanates from its history and culture. (Akoto, 1992, p. 46)

Jegna - is a translation from the ancient kingdom of Abyssinian. In the African culture, jegna is a title of distinction. The word *jegna* has been translated into English as hero, warrior, soldier, courage, strength and protection of our culture, land, people, and elders (The Association of Black Psychologists (https://abpsi.org/national-programs/).

Reference

Akoto, K. (1992). *Nationbuilding: Theory and practice in Afrikan-centered education*. African World Press.

Du Bois, W. E. B. (2008). *The souls of black folk* (B. H. Edwards, Ed.). Oxford University Press. (Original work published 1903)

The Association of Black Psychologists. (2022). *Jegnaship and Training*. Retrieved August 8, 2022, from https://abpsi.org/national-programs/

PART I

ABEN - THE FOUNDATION

ONE

The Making of the Vision

Rona M. Frederick, PhD

A prayer to our ancestors: A libation[1]

When we call on our ancestors, they show up in the situation in us and as us.
We call on our ancestors and all of those who are watching over us. We invoke their presence and ask them to be with us in this space, and, in this time and in our work.
In this moment we need the power and insight of our ancestors to show up in this situation
To show up in our current situation and Black education and us.
So, I will begin by calling on Baba Asa G. Hilliard
We miss you here, so much
But we know you have not left us. We know that if we call on you, you will show up in us—(as us.
We call on Dr Lorraine Monroe who we recently lost in 2018.
We need your mind, we need your sharpness
We need your strength, we need your endurance
We call on Marva Collins . . . we call on your courage
We call on Mama Barbara Sizemore . . .
We call on you to be with us to show up in us as us.
Your clarity, your courage, your unwavering love for Black children.
We call you to show up in our situation to show up in us as us, Barbara Sizemore- Ashe!
We call on Baba James Baldwin.
You always spoke courageously about what our children needed.
We call on WEB Dubois.
We call on your clarity, we call on your love for the Black intellectual tradition,
We call on you to show up.
We call on Mama Zora Neale Hurston, we call on you to show up in us,
You spoke out against desegregation.
Nannie Helen Burroughs, Ashe
Mary Mcleod Bethune, Ashe
Anna Julia Cooper, Ashe
Baba Carter G Woodson, Ashe!
Show up in us as us
Ashe, Ashe, Ashe!

(Lesesne, 2021, Libation, ABEN Institute)

In June 2021, amid the COVID-19 Pandemic, 146 educators gathered on ZOOM to commence the 16th Summer Institute of A Black Education Network (ABEN). Debra Watkins, ABEN's founder, like an energetic ray of sunshine, called the excited audience to attention. The chat was abuzz with greetings from all over the country. Although virtual, the anticipation was palpable.

Joyce King, internationally recognized for her leadership and research in and around racial equity in education and culturally centered thought, set the stage for the two-day Institute by framing the importance and intentionality behind its African epistemology. Deliberate in her words of wisdom, remembrance, and action, in the opening speech to the audience of educators, community members, and organizers she shared that we "mistakenly believe that there is no cultural heritage intact as a foundation for [Black] resilience and excellence." She warned, "Be aware of distraction—read the social and political landscape." She lovingly reminded the captive group that in the words of Nkulu N-Zhenga, "knowledge is not merely a right. With knowledge comes the responsibility to care for others and for the world. Knowledge in African epistemology is the path to becoming fully human and humane." She closed with a message given to her by Baba Asa Hilliard, a luminary in African-centered education and psychology, who reminded us of the work ahead, from the book *Osiris Rising* [passage taken from *Black Education*, pg. 350]: "For we intend, as Africans, to retrieve our human face, our human heart, the human mind our ancestors taught to sour. That is who we are and why" (King, 2021). With those words from the brilliant elder, the Institute began.

Much like the Nile River, which has been a vital source of irrigation for African villages to transform dry land into lush, fertile ground, ABEN serves as a metaphoric watering hole where Black educators gather to nourish, connect, and most importantly, renew their spirits as they pour knowledge into Black children in their own communities nationally and abroad. ABEN, which in the Songhoy language of Mali means "the buck stops here," is a movement for and by Black educators with the goal of reversing the backward slide by fostering spaces for Black excellence by designing or eking out high quality experiences for Black youth, teachers, community activists, and schools. Its fearless leader and former Master teacher, Debra Watkins, serves as Executive Director of ABEN.

For nearly 20 years, educators have convened at one of the signature programs of ABEN, the Summer Institute. They come together in California to commune, plan, strategize, connect, and reflect on how they will foster spaces of Black educational excellence in their community. They come by themselves, as parents, or as a community, with the divine purposes of being fortified, of creating systems, and of carrying the knowledge, resources, and newly formed networks back to their community.

In 2021, Black educators came at a time when the world was slowly realizing the relentless attacks and lynchings on the Black body through the death of George Floyd and countless others—a reality that has lived in the fabric of most Black people's DNA since the beginning of their involuntary status in the United States. They gather at a time when widespread policy is being crafted to ban racialized conversations and curriculum in K-12 schools. As Joyce King declared at the 16th Institute, ABEN offers a safe space to renew and remember.

The context of resistance and racialized combat is not new. Members of the African community, particularly Black children, have been under siege since their presence in the United States. Policy, schools, and teachers systematically maintain institutions that serve to dehumanize and mute the voices of Black children.

History is replete with such examples. Lily Ann Granderson, an enslaved African, established a "midnight" school in the early 1800s for the children in Mississippi where literacy of slaves was prohibited, and worked clandestinely through the night at the risk of severe punishment to teach hundreds to read and write (Brookland Museum, n.d.). Marva Collins, a teacher disgruntled with Chicago schools, single-handedly raised test scores five grade levels when she opened her home in 1975 to teach children in her neighborhood (Collins, 2003). ABEN offers a counter pathway to the ongoing colonization of the Black community in the United States in the 21st century. In both formal and informal ways, ABEN works around and through the monstrosities called racism and White supremacy by providing tunnels and safe havens for African educators to coalesce, to share both deep thought and educational excellence. It is a space for them to become fortified to transform the life experiences of Black children and communities. This is done through intentional relationship-building, the elevation of Black scholarship, and strategic planning. All conversations are framed by an African-centered consciousness embodying the goal of Black liberation. As important, Debra Watkins provides funding, space for rich conversations and action planning, and opportunities for Black entrepreneurship to market both their products and curriculum.

Clarity around what must be done to liberate Black children has been central to ABEN's vision since its inception. Its mission is to reverse the backward slide by utilizing culturally informed research, technology, and visionary community networking within the African diaspora to facilitate academic and cultural excellence wherever our scholars are.

Debra Watkins, the founder of ABEN, finds the treatment of African people in the United States to be egregious, and reflected that:

> The underachievement of Black children and historic marginalization is criminal. It feels criminal to me, you know, that Black children have been historically marginalized for four hundred years in this country. We weren't even allowed to read or write for most of those years (D. Watkins, personal communications, June 22, 2021).

She rests confidently in the knowledge that communities of African descent across the world derive from a rich cultural legacy—prior to colonialism—that is often misunderstood or unknown. To tell the history of Africans in America, she would argue, one must begin at the source; the continent of Africa where great educators like Imhotep and institutions like the University of Sankore derive. Knowing the rich legacy of communities of African descent, Debra Watkins' philosophy is simple but poignant: Instead of wringing our hands about what to do to help Black and Brown students succeed in schools that were never designed for them, why not as a community foster and connect spaces of and for Black excellence? This belief has driven both ABEN and its mother organization, the California Alliance of African American Educations (CAAAE), which has been self-determining and taking collective responsibility for the outcomes of Black children for the past 20 years. Today, the CAAAE has morphed into a national network that is rapidly attracting an audience. From humble beginnings, it currently boasts an impressive track record, garnering over $10 million in support of its overall goals of Black excellence, self-knowledge, and achievement for Black youth. Most importantly, ABEN, through its programming and philanthropy, has touched the lives of tens of thousands of youth, educators, and community members.

The Context

Many Black educators have historically struggled against racist policies and an oppressive sociopolitical context to instill a sense of love of self and culture, to promote academic excellence, and to design liberatory spaces for Black youth. According to Watkins, disparities in African American educational achievement began during enslavement when Africans were forbidden to read and write. Yet many Africans used clandestine methods to educate themselves: Resistance and resilience were always at play while Europeans attempted to quell the life and spirit of African people.

Throughout the 19th and 20th centuries, self-education and self-reliance held true especially for the Black community and Black teachers throughout the South. People of African descent built their own educational institutions in an attempt to self-educate. Despite adversities, members of the Black community have both resisted and rejected hegemonic practices of the dominant culture while facing persistent and profound barriers to educational opportunity. To be clear, education has always been equated to liberation for Black communities. In his book, *The Education of Blacks in the South* (1988), James Anderson captures the Black community's belief in the power of education. He stated that when compared to other ethnic groups in the United States, African Americans had the greatest literacy gains in the shortest period of time. Only 7% of African Americans were literate in 1863. By 1950, despite school segregation and unequal access to resources, the literacy rate jumped to 90% (Anderson, 1988).

Despite segregation, forced integration, and education policies designed to eradicate the "opportunity gap," many members of the Black community are well aware of systemic racism and structural racism that blankets the experiences of many Black children in schools. In retrospect, *Brown vs. Board of Education* (1954) policy led to droves of Master Black teachers losing their jobs during integration, the loss of community-controlled schools, and the integration of Black children into non-Black schools (Siddle Walker, 2018). Many would argue that these integrated U.S. schools, in their form and function, led to an unfulfilled promise that did not support the academic achievement for Black children.

In his text, *Too Much Schooling, Too Little Education* (1994), Shujaa argues that the school system is doing exactly what it is designed to do, "to perpetuate and maintain society's existing power relations and institutional structures that support that arrangement" (p. 15). He points out that one must simply look at the leadership to understand the "concept, values, and skills" that schools transmit. In the case of schooling in the United States, White, Anglo-Saxon, Protestant values inculcate the schooling system. On the other hand, Shujaa makes a clear distinction between education and schooling. He argues that education is the process of transmitting the "knowledge of the values, aesthetics, spiritual beliefs, and all things that give a particular cultural orientation its uniqueness" (p.15). Although there are some skills to be gained by matriculation through the U.S. school system, for Black children, knowledge of self, knowledge of one's rich history, knowledge that our children are both divine gifts of the creator and tools for institution and nationbuilding, must come from within and require a "collective worldview" (p.15).

Debra Watkins' design and formulation of several thriving Black institutions dedicated to liberatory practices for Black youth reflects the importance of ABEN's holding the space for Black children and Black organizers working within and outside of the U.S. schooling systems. Much like the rise of the independent Catholic schooling system in the 1800s, the inspiration for ABEN comes from the strong desire to both self-educate and educate for freedom as well as to bring together those freedom fighters whose mission is to do the same. Institution-building and nation-building is at the heart of ABEN, whose goal is to carry on the legacy of the myriads of heroes, known and unknown, who sought to maintain the deep respect of ancestors and community traditions, to facilitate intergenerational cultural transmission, and to strive for the highest standards in science and technology.

Watkins, like her ancestors, sees herself as part of a long line of resistors whose main goal is to bring forth the brilliance of Black children. This is her story and the story of ABEN: One educator with a mission to organically transform the trajectory for Black students one person at a time.

Setting the Stage

ABEN began in California as the California Alliance of African American Educators (CAAAE). For many, California is referred to as "The Golden State," symbolizing the Gold Rush and the beautiful fields of yellow poppies that bloom each spring. The state boasts the possibility of wealth and opportunity, and prides itself on diversity because it serves as a natural entryway to and from Mexico.

For Blacks, California became a natural attractor during the Great Migration. As African Americans flooded the cities of Washington, D.C., New York, and Chicago, they also headed West to California. Like many, Debra Watkins' mother came to Los Angeles at the age of 12 in 1935 and later settled in Compton until moving to Pomona to provide opportunity for their family.

Despite California's reputation as both a pioneer for academic freedom and for episodic revolutionary activism—as evidenced by San Francisco State's establishment of the first Black studies department in 1968; the founding of organizations such as the Black Panther Party; and the work of the US Organization—the lived experiences of many Black residents have not been so golden.

From the 1850s to the late 1940s, courts and laws across the United States supported discriminatory housing practices and the exclusion and segregation of Black students in and from school. For example, in 1852, California's fugitive slave law banned Black children from California public schools, even though California was nominally a free state (Moore, 2022).

In *Ward v. Flood* (1874), which preceded *Plessy v. Ferguson* (1896), the California Supreme Court upheld segregation as "separate but equal" and supported a public school's refusal to admit a Black child (EdTrust-West, 2015). In 1947, the state ruled against segregated schools after a public school did not admit a Mexican American student. This groundbreaking case, *Mendez v. Westminster School District*, struck down racialized school segregation in California, prompted the California Legislature to repeal school segregation laws, and laid the groundwork for *Brown v. Board of Education* in 1954. The Education Trust-West report, entitled *Black Minds Matter*, adds that de facto segregation continued due to both the lack of systemic efforts to desegregate and the continuous discriminatory housing practices (EdTrust-West, 2015).

In many Black communities, parents criticized the overcrowded classrooms and dilapidated school buildings. This held true especially for San Francisco Bay area schools, which commonly practiced de facto segregation well into the 1960s.

The 1960s saw the rise of self-help efforts in California in the form of African-centered schools. These schools could be considered one of a long line of institutions built by and for the Black community to sustain self-reliance and ownership over the curriculum. Six such independent Afrocentric community schools were established in African American communities in California during this period: the Nairobi Day School, founded in East Palo

Alto in 1966; the Afro-American School of Culture, founded in Los Angeles in 1967; Omowale Ujamaa of Pasadena, founded in 1973; the Winnie Mandela Children's Learning Village, established in Compton in 1973; the Marcus Garvey School of Los Angeles, founded in 1975; and Uhuru Shule, founded in Los Angeles in 1978 (Kifano, 1996).

In 1974, the U.S. Supreme Court ruled on the *Milliken v. Bradley* case, barring desegregation across school district lines. Like many cities across the nation, the impact caused White flight as families fled to affluent suburban counties. The push to integrate, paradoxically, served to exacerbate the already fragile inequitable social and economic conditions pervasive throughout California (EdTrust-West, 2015).

Adequate funding for schools also created barriers to schooling. Proposition 13, passed in 1978, capped the local property taxes available to fund California schools, leaving one to question the value of public education in general for its residents. Foster (1996) cited that in 1994, California trailed behind most schools, spending more than "$1000 less than the national average and nearly $3000 less than the per student expenditure in New York" (p. 107).

In higher education, Proposition 209 ended affirmative action in all of California's public institutions. The policy timeline presented by Education Trust-West cited that, "as a result, between 1995 and 1998, the number of African American, Latino, and Native American students dropped by 58% at the University of California, Berkeley and 53% at University of California, Los Angeles" (EdTrust-West, 2015).

According to the California Educational Statistics, Foster (1996) adds that in the 1990s, there were fewer than 12,000 African American teachers in California, on the K-12 level, representing 5.1% of teachers statewide.

She also notes that:

> In San Francisco, 49% of African American students scored in the lowest quartile on District-wide tests in both reading and math (Wagner, 1996). In Oakland, the median grade point average for Black students was 1.8 on a 4.0 scale—the lowest of any ethnic group (Fields, 1997). Moreover, Black students were retained at higher rates, 64% and represented 80% of suspended students (p. 106).

By 1999, California passed the Public Schools Accountability Act to hold each California school responsible for the academic achievement of all students, including subgroups (EdTrust-West, 2015). Two years later, the Federal No Child Left Behind Act of 2001 also required that states report data for each subgroup and required action if schools weren't making progress toward targets. The idea was to disseminate funding for special populations in need. However, according to one administrator, in many suburbs in California, such as Alameda County where the population of Black youth is low, Black students did not reach the minimum threshold to be counted, which begs a discussion around funding for Black students.

Where is the Funding and Support for Black Children in California?

California has always been at the forefront of the highly politicized debate around immigration and language in the United States. As important, the questions of where and with whom financial resources will be placed continue to be a hotbed of discussion. Black community members, families, and teachers often complain that the specific cultural needs of African American students in California are often marginalized in policy discussion around literacy and equity.

In 1994, led by Noma LeMoine, the Los Angeles School District embarked on an innovative literacy program for elementary students designed to boost the academic achievement of Black students, particularly those who live in segregated, and often linguistically isolated, neighborhoods. LeMoine made an important distinction between English language learners (ELLs) and standard English learners (SELs). SELs are a distinct group of students who speak languages that do not correspond to standard American English structure and grammar but that incorporate English vocabulary (LeMoine & Soto, 2017). This includes African Americans who speak African American English. LeMoine argues that both the ELLs and the SELs need instructional support to successfully access the school curriculum.

The purpose of the Academic English Mastery Program was to provide teachers with professional development and specific strategies to support their students in distinguishing between African American language and mainstream English. Of great import was engaging students in the discussion of when to use what language. LeMoine, along with several other linguists, maintained that the language used by many Black students is rooted in the African languages of the Niger-Congo region. The two languages share many basic grammatical rules (Schnaiberg,1994). The enslaved Africans taken from that region were prohibited from using their native tongues so they adopted the English vocabulary. But because they were never taught "standard English," they continued to lay those English words on top of African structures.

Proponents of Ebonics would argue that these linguistic patterns have been passed down for decades to today's generation of African Americans. Therefore, intentional instruction to teach Black children the rules of standard English was necessary. Most importantly, children learned to switch between the two languages while still honoring their home language. Teachers learned the invaluable lesson to not lower expectations for Black children based on the way they spoke. Black parents advocated on behalf of their children, wanting money used for bilingual education to support this programming. The school district budgeted resources annually to support the initiative—none of which came from federal funds.

The Los Angeles program sent nearly 1,000 teachers and 600 paraprofessionals, mostly non-African Americans, through various seminars, courses, workshops, and conferences on language and cultural issues. For 20 years, Dr. LeMoine served as Director of the Los Angeles Unified School District's Academic English Mastery Program that supported teachers, administrators, and paraeducators in effectively incorporating culturally and linguistically responsive pedagogy into core instruction. This program became an antidote for cultural mismatch in the classroom by embodying the following beliefs:

1. Instruction must be culturally relevant and linguistically responsive in order for SELs to access a standards-based curriculum.
2. The history, culture, experiences, and canons of literature of SELs must be infused into the learning environment and instructional design.
3. Strategies must be used to support the acquisition of school language and literacy.
4. Teachers must build on the cultural learning and strengths of the SELs with supports and scaffolds to allow access to rigorous core curriculum (LeMoine & Soto, 2017).

Under Dr. LeMoine's visionary leadership, the Academic English Mastery Program became a national model for addressing the language, literacy, and learning needs of African American and other students for whom standard English is not native. More specifically, the program supported classroom teachers by incorporating instructional strategies into the curriculum. These instructional strategies were designed to facilitate the acquisition of standard and academic English in classroom environments that validate, value, and build upon the language and culture of the students (LAUSD, n.d.).

On December 18, 1996, the Oakland Unified School District in California passed what was deemed a "controversial resolution" recognizing the legitimacy of Ebonics—what mainstream linguists more commonly term African American English (AAE)—as an African language. The resolution set off a firestorm of media criticism and ignited a national debate. The dominant narrative soon took shape that Oakland was trying to "dumb down" education by accepting Black English as a legitimate language of its own, and even teaching it to students. Maya Angelou and other celebrities and linguists became involved in the debate, debunking the very notion of teaching Ebonics.

After a Congressional hearing, Oakland released an updated resolution that removed every mention of the word Ebonics and ended the Academic English Mastery Program in many schools. Although there are still a few schools that continue to use what has been deemed in retrospect a very successful program, the program largely disbanded after LeMoine's retirement in 2009.

In 2017, Hobbes, senior writer for the *Huff Post*, revisited this debate and shares:

> But what the last 20 years have demonstrated . . . is the sheer scale of the missed opportunity. America's out-of-hand dismissal of AAVE [African-American Vernacular English] has widened the racial achievement gap, entrenched discrimination, and made us all a little more scared of each other. Which raises the simple question: What's keeping us from making another push for AAVE now?

One Oakland school administrator recalled that after the Ebonics controversy, money dedicated to her Black students disappeared. She received a call from the school district saying they were pulling the funding and instead, distributing the money to bilingual programs serving ELLs. The administrator openly resisted. Although her school rebounded due to her resourcefulness (and kept all of their assistance), this began the trend of Title 1 funding being largely diverted away from Black students to their bilingual counterparts. Debra Watkins notes that when LeMoine retired [in 2009], they dismantled the program, essentially, so that there might be maybe 10 schools left using the model. The focus of the school district, whether financial, curricular, or otherwise, shifted to non-Black language learners.

Debra Watkins maintains that this is "why Black children tend to underperform in [California] schools: They don't feel cared about and valued." One of the greatest challenges faced by many Black youth in California is access to necessary culturally responsive resources.

California's Black Educators

"When a needle falls into a well, many people will look into the well, but only a few will be ready to go down after it" (African proverb).

In the past 40 years, education scholars re-present stories about liberatory Black teachers. By doing this, they capture the spectrum of differences among Black teachers with hopes of countering the one-dimensional image that historically dominated the literature. These stories represent the complex experiences that many Black teachers faced within a raced, gendered, and classed environment (Foster, 1996; Fultz, 1995; McGhee, 2019) and are used to demonstrate attributes such as "othermothering," caring, organizing, leading, and holding high expectations for their Black students.

These stories disclose the ongoing sacrifices, resistance, and struggle Black teachers experienced in their efforts to demand quality education for Black students (Anderson, 1988; Shujaa, 1994). These stories capture the trauma of racialized isolation, colleague fatigue, and reconceptualization of miseducation in the curriculum. These stories, tied to larger stories of oppression, resistance, and liberation, provide a voice for those historically marginalized in the literature and demonstrate how teachers acted as double agents to manipulate the system to empower their Black students. These stories also tell how Black teachers work outside the system or in clandestine ways recognizing that "we must teach our own" (Akoto, 1992; Shujaa, 1994).

More recently, these representations capture the antiracist practices of Black teachers by demonstrating culturally responsive (Ball, 2000; Ladson-Billings, 1994); emancipatory teaching practices (Lynn, 2006); abolitionist (Love, 2019); and fugitive pedagogies (Givens, 2021). Taken in total, these stories seek to contribute to the growing body of literature that portrays the countless dimensions of Black teachers, their experiences, and their liberatory practices within a racially oppressive institution. Many of these teachers consciously and deliberately subvert the dominant perception that African children are unlovable, unteachable, second-class citizens who are limited to narrow life outcomes rather than focusing on moral uplift.

Many of those California Black teachers initially attracted to CAAAE/ ABEN worked in anti-Black spaces with low percentages of Black colleagues and students. Being one of a few in their schools and school districts, they struggled daily with micro and macroaggressions. An ABEN participant of more than 20 years shared her experiences in Alameda County, California:

> The racism in schools was palpable. There were only two Black teachers and they both shared that they often found racist literature in their mailboxes. I also observed that there were only five Black boys in the school, and they spent the majority of the school day sitting in the front office missing out on classroom instruction (B. Brooks, personal communication, July 19, 2021).

To be clear, these consistent attacks were not uncommon. Racial battle fatigue (RBF) refers to the psychological, emotional, and physiological toll of confronting racism daily (Smith, 2004). In schools, this includes daily interactions with colleagues and systemic structures like tracking and discipline procedures that preclude children from having full access to the curriculum; lack of acknowledgement; miseducation of curriculum; and the isolation associated with being the lone ranger designing liberatory spaces for Black children in an anti-Black establishment.

She continued to comment on the drastic differences between being teacher, and later as an administrator in Hayward Unified School District (HUSD) in the '90s. In Oakland, she was working with a predominantly Black staff. In Alameda, the demographics shifted to all White for teachers and students alike. She shared:

> I was the only Black teacher . . . and I noticed that [in general] there was only one Black teacher or two Black teachers [in neighboring schools] and they were so, so, so isolated. I know I felt isolated, I felt like I had no one to turn to. I wanted to have support and mentorship. [I] also knew that parents and teachers felt alone in the plight to support Black students in these schools.
>
> She recalled that a group of African American staff decided to start a Black educator's group that included both certified and classified staff and discovered

> that there were fewer than 20 African Americans meeting those criteria in the entire district (B. Brooks, personal communication, July 19, 2021).

In addition to the need to connect, CAAAE participants also shared that those Black teachers present may or may not have operated with the understanding or desire to commit to the academic achievement of Black children. In fact, some held the same misguided beliefs of low expectations and negative stereotypes. For example, DeGruy (2017) theorizes racialized socialization as the adoption of the attitudes, values, and views of White superiority. People, things, and ideas associated with European Americans are taught and thought to be better, more intelligent, and overall, more desirable. From the inception of the slave trade, African Americans were taught to see Black characteristics, religion, vernacular, and people as inferior and not to be valued. In addition, White standards including beauty, material success, and denial of the significance of Black history, have been adopted by many African Americans trying to assimilate to this culture. Thus, when Black teachers are physically present in schools, there is no guarantee that their presence will support the racial uplift of their community or liberation for Black children; thus, there is a need to create distance for those conscious Black teachers who strive toward community improvement.

One parent and grassroots organizer who was drawn to ABEN shed light on his search for support when his young son entered first grade in the suburban schools in Alameda County where conscious Black teachers were far and few between. He shared that it was "as if [his son] had the weight of the world on his shoulders. He did not look or feel that way until he got into public education." In a sense, they noticed their son slowly getting the life sucked out of him. They shared that "they had personally faced 'the boogie man' head on and knew that something needed to be done." He added:

> I was a man searching trying to find answers. Where is my army? . . . if I have to fight this thing myself and go to the school board meeting [I will] . . . but I know there has got to be a more efficient way (M. Gaskins, personal communication, May 20, 2021).

Thus, for many conscious educators, parents, and grassroots organizers, racial isolation and battle fatigue became a driver to organize and to find their army. The CAAAE, which would eventually become ABEN, became their home base.

Through word of mouth, kindred spirits committed to the larger mission of liberation of Black children were attracted to CAAAE. Its Institutes and professional development breakfasts offered safety, edification, and healing; Debra Watkins provided the spark and the sage, and the CAAAE programming became aspirational for Black educators across the state.

Questions

Research the history of Black education in your district. Compare and contrast policy and innovation in your place of residence with that of California.

Note

1. A Libation is a West African tradition when we call on our ancestors, evoke their presence, and ask them to be present.

References

Akoto, K. (1992). *Nationbuilding: Theory and practice in Afrikan-centered education*. African World Press.

Anderson, J. D. (1988). *Education of Blacks in the South, 1860–1935*. The University of North Carolina Press.

Armah, A. K. (1995). *Osiris rising: A novel of African past, present and future*. Per Ankh Press.

Ball, A. F. (2000). Empowering pedagogies that enhance the learning of multicultural students. *Teachers College Record, 102*(6), 1006–1034. https://doi.org/ 10.1111/0161-4681.00090

Brookland Museum. (n.d.). Milla Granson. https://www.brooklynmuseum.org/eascfa/dinner_party/heritage_floor/milla_granson

Collins, P. (2003). *The school that cared: A story of the Marva Collins Preparatory School of Cincinnati*. University Press of America.

DeGruy, J. A. (2017). *Post traumatic slave syndrome: American's legacy of enduring injury and healing* (Rev. ed.). Joy DeGruy Publications Inc.

EdTrust-West. (2015). *Black minds matter: The educational success of Black children in California*. https://west.edtrust.org/resource/black-minds-matter-supporting-the-educational-success-of-black-children-in-california/

Foster, M. (1996). As California goes, so goes the nation. *The Journal of Negro Education, 65*(2), 105–110.

Fultz, M. (1995). African American teachers in the South, 1890–1940: Powerlessness and the ironies of expectations and protest. *History of Education Quarterly, 35*(4), 401–422. https://doi.org/10.2307/369578

Givens, J. R. (2021). *Fugitive pedagogy: Carter G. Woodson and the art of Black teaching.* Harvard University Press.

Hobbes, M. (2017). Why America needs Ebonics now. *Highline Huffington Post.* https://highline.huffingtonpost.com/articles/en/ebonics/

Kifano, S. (1996). Afrocentric education in supplementary schools: Paradigm and practice at the Mary McLeod Bethune Institute. *The Journal of Negro Education, 65*(2), 209–218. https://doi.org/10.2307/2967314

King, J. E. (Ed.). (2005). *Black education: A transformative research and action agenda for the new century.* Routledge.

King, J. E. (2021, June 14-15). Introductory Remarks [Speech]. ABEN Summer Institute.

Ladson-Billings, G. (1994). *The dreamkeepers: Successful teachers of African American children* (1st ed.). Jossey-Bass Publishers.

Lesesne, A. (2021). *Libation.* ABEN Institute.

LeMoine, N., & Soto, I. (2017). *Academic language mastery: Culture in context.* Corwin.

Los Angeles Unified School District (LAUSD). (n.d.). The Academic English Mastery Program (AEMP). https://achieve.lausd.net/AEMP

Love, B. L. (2019). *We want to do more than survive: Abolitionist teaching and the pursuit of educational freedom.* Beacon Press.

Lynn, M. (2006). Education for the community: Exploring the culturally relevant practices of Black male teachers. *Teachers College Record, 108*(12), 2497–2522. https://doi.org/10.1111/j.1467-9620.2006.00792.x

McGhee, C., & Anderson, G. (2019). Gentrification, market regimes, and the new entrepreneurial principal: Enacting integration or displacement? *Leadership and Policy in Schools, 18*(2), 180–194.

Moore, S. (2022). *Chapter 1: Race, slavery, and freedom - The nature of freedom in the West.* https://www.nps.gov/articles/000/chapter-1-race-slavery-and-freedom-the-nature-of-freedom-in-the-west

Shujaa, M. (1994). *Too much schooling, too little education: A paradox of Black life in White societies.* African World Press.

Smith, J. L. (2004). Understanding the process of stereotype threat: A review of mediational variables and new performance goal directions. *Educational Psychology Review, 16*(3), 177–206. https://doi.org/10.1023/B:EDPR.0000034020.20317.89

Schnaiberg, L. (1994). Talking the talk. *Education Week.* https://www.edweek.org/education/talking-the-talk/1994/10

Siddle Walker, V. (2018). *The lost education of Horace Tate: Uncovering the hidden heroes who fought for justice in schools.* The New Press.

TWO

ABEN – Reimagining Black Education

Rona M. Frederick, PhD

When one is in a struggle or battle, he looks around to see if he is alone.

—*Charles Moody, NABSE*

THE HISTORY AND JOURNEY OF the Black-led, Black-run organization CAAAE, which would become ABEN, is for many an untold story. Beginning in the 1980s, Debra Watkins, one courageous school teacher with a clear mission, set forth to build bridges and pathways for freedom fighters who would, in turn, transform the minds and spirits of children of African ancestry in California schools. The story begins with the Santa Clara County Alliance of Black Educators (SCCABE) and with its parent organization, the National Alliance of Black School Educators (NABSE).

The Beginning

Figure 2.1. Santa Clara County Alliance of Black Educators.

In 1970, Dr. Charles D. Moody, Sr. invited several African American superintendents to a meeting at the O'Hare Marriott Hotel in Chicago, Illinois. The purpose of the meeting was to share concerns, to develop a resource pool, and to form an organization to support Black education. A year later, the group met again in Miami Beach, Florida and organized the National Alliance of Black School Superintendents (NABSS); Dr. Russell Jackson was duly elected President (NABSE, n.d.).

In 1973, three years later, NABSS voted to expand the organization to include administrators and other educational personnel. The name was officially changed from NABSS to the National Alliance of Black School Educators (NABSE), with special attention paid to linking "members with common and related job functions." NABSE officially launched on November 23, 1973 in Detroit, Michigan, with 284 charter members and a mission of "furthering the academic success for the nation's children, particularly children of African descent" (NABSE, n.d.).

NABSE developed during a time when Blacks were reeling from the consequences of integration and when misguided assertions regarding the genetic inferiority of the Black race were rife. It emerged at a time where many Black communities were organizing and looking for community control. Simultaneously, Black teachers working in U.S. schools were desiring a space to coalesce and organize on behalf of their students.

NABSE's organizational structure offered Black educators across the nation an opportunity to formulate local and regional chapters. Thirteen years after the inception of NABSE, Debra Watkins became a founding member of the Santa Clara County Alliance of Black Educators (SCCABE), one of NABSE's affiliates. Located in a wealthy county of Northern California, Santa Clara, also known as Silicon Valley, it is best known as an incubator for global technology companies. Santa Clara is the birthplace of computer giants including Apple, Facebook, and Google. It was also a space where Black teachers yearned for support and a like-minded community.

For Debra Watkins, the NABSE affiliation allowed her to yield more influence in ensuring educational achievement for Black children, particularly in designing a K-16 pipeline into college prep courses in the Silicon Valley community colleges and universities. SCCABE offered the few Black educators in the area the opportunity to connect with one another and to listen to distinguished African American keynote speakers and panelists. They held awards ceremonies to celebrate Black children transitioning from fifth, eighth, and 12th grade. Although the organization never had a robust budget, the ceremonies attracted hundreds of parents and community members and became a model for other school districts, like Alameda, that wanted to acknowledge the educational achievements of their Black youth (Watkins, 2016).

Being a local leader of NABSE allowed Debra to engage with other affiliate leaders in California and across the nation. One special relationship developed between Debra Watkins and James Taylor, president of the San Francisco Alliance of Black School Educators. At the time, Taylor served as a well-respected principal of Dr. Martin Luther King, Jr. Middle School in San Francisco and was considered a pillar in his community. Debra Watkins shared that they saw each other at the annual NABSE conferences for 20 years. Together, they "sat at the feet of Asa Hilliard and Barbara Sizemore" and never missed a conference. He would become a natural ally and much needed advisor when Debra Watkins decided it was time to take her affiliation with NABSE to a statewide level.

As her concerns for Black children's educational achievement in California grew, Watkins began working with affiliates to establish a statewide organization. In 1998, she consulted with Taylor, who by then was a friend and colleague, and Ellen Posey, president of Oakland Alliance of Black Educators. The trio met several times for approximately one year in Burlingame, midpoint between San Jose, Oakland, and San Francisco, to discuss their vision for the statewide organization. The goal was to bring Black educators together to support, strategize, and change the trajectory of Black students in California's schools. Tragically, Ellen succumbed to cancer and the partnership paused for a year while grieving the loss. Honoring Ellen's legacy, the group reconvened with Clifford Thompson, the new president of the Oakland Alliance of Black School Educators, and Lynne Murray, a teacher colleague and officer in Debra Watkins' organization. Later, Debra Watkins added William Ellerbee, an administrator for the Sacramento Unified School District.

Debra Watkins immediately asked James Taylor to serve in the role of vice president. He, in turn, encouraged Debra Watkins to think strategically. He suggested there should be six regions, and each region in California should be assigned a membership coordinator. Each regional coordinator would commit to its mission and grow the organization.

Following his sage advice, Debra Watkins began reaching out to the CA affiliates to invite them to serve as board members from the Valley Region, Sacramento, San Diego, and Los Angeles. This was a model that would serve CAAAE/ABEN well over the years as it allowed for regional representatives to have autonomy while also growing the network.

While Watkins was organizing the statewide California organization with the goal of officially affiliating with NABSE, NABSE experienced an internal crisis. Members of the organization began questioning the history of its founding. As a result, a schism fractured the organization, leading to its members being encouraged to "pick a side."

Simultaneously, excited by the opportunity for CAAAE to become a charter affiliate of NABSE and to hold statewide distinction, Debra Watkins put in an application to become a charter statewide affiliate of NABSE. With their list of officers, six regions, and coordinators in place, and all of their commissions in order, CAAAE was on the verge of being approved.

Unbeknownst to Debra Watkins, another member of NABSE, who was deeply entrenched in the NABSE's founders' debate, decided to resurrect her former organization, the California Alliance of Black School Educators (CABSE). Although CABSE had been defunct for 15 years, this member insisted in securing NABSE's approval of her application. NABSE launched an investigation to see whose application came in first. Unable to determine, NABSE asked the two leaders to work together. The other member chose not to collaborate. As a result, Debra Watkins and her board decided to no longer contest CABSE's claims and officially started their own organization with executive-level representation from all of NABSE's affiliates at the time except the one in Los Angeles. The name selected was the California Alliance of African American Educators (CAAAE).

The CAAAE began in October, 2001 with two goals. First, informing and inspiring educators with proven pedagogical resources to ensure academic and cultural excellence for students of African ancestry. Second, providing services to students and families in order to create culturally conscious African Americans who are lifelong learners and critical thinkers.

The California Alliance of African American Educators (CAAAE)

While still working full time as a teacher for the East Side Union High School District, Debra Watkins and her committed founding board members built

Figure 2.2. CAAAE.

the California Alliance from the ground up. Debra Watkins launched its Summer Institutes at Stanford University that focused on professional development for teachers and on designing STEM programs such as the Frank S. Greene Scholars Program for the youth. Over the next 10 years, the Institutes combined to serve more than 1,000 educators. Evaluations taken each year demonstrated that the speakers were well received and that the format empowered educators to go back to their communities inspired, supported, and equipped with the necessary resources to fight on behalf of their Black youth.

Although the STEM programming continued, the CAAAE Summer Institutes paused in their 11th year. Debra Watkins approached the CAAAE Board to recommend that they pivot to focus on advocacy. Being an adaptive leader, her desire was to position CAAAE in ways that would influence statewide policies and practices. Of import were three policy issues that served to undermine Black education; teacher credentialing, school discipline and the school-to prison pipeline, and the local control funding formula (LCFF), a policy issue in which her colleague, Linda Darling-Hammond was engaged. As a result, Debra Watkins joined several statewide committees. CAAAE partnered with Fix School Discipline, an organization designed to dismantle the California school-to-prison pipeline while supporting an agenda to improve teacher credentialing.

A BRIEF HISTORY OF

STANFORD INSTITUTES KEYNOTE SPEAKERS

2002
Bob Moses – The Algebra Project

2003
Beverly Tatum – Author, *Why are all the Black Kids Sitting Together in the Cafeteria and other conversations about race*

2004
Gloria Ladson Billings – coined the term "Culturally Relevant Teaching" and first applied the term Critical Race Theory to education.

2005
Pedro Noguera – Author, *City Schools and the American Dream: Fulfilling the Promise of Public Education*

2006
African Centered Superstar Scholars – Dr. Wade Nobles, internationally-renowned psychologist in the field of African Psychology; Joyce King, then author of the seminal book entitled Black Education; and Noma Lemoine, then director of the Academic English Mastery Program in Los Angeles.

2007
Lisa Delpit – Author, *The Silenced Dialogue: Power and Pedagogy in Educating Other People's Children*

2008
Sharroky Hollie – co-founder of the Culture and Language Academy of Success (CLAS) in Los Angeles and highly sought after professional developer in culturally responsive teaching.

2009
Bob Moses returns!

2010
Carol Lee, African centered scholar best known for her work in "cultural modeling"

2011
Geneva Gay – Author, *Culturally Responsive Teaching: Theory, Practice and Research*

Figure 2.3. ABEN Institute Keynote Speakers.

Debra Watkins is unwilling to back down, making local and state educational ecosystems more responsive to the needs of Black students and families became a larger goal. Building out an independent school system by and for the Black community soon became the vision.

Reimagining Black Education: A Black Education Network

As CAAAE was moving into the policy realm, Joyce King worked alongside Debra Watkins and began to reimagine education for Black children. Joyce King is considered by many to be a leader in advancing educational research and practical application for Black youth. In 2005, she edited one of the most definitive books entitled, *Black Education: A Transformative Research and Action Agenda for The New Century*. Consistent with her life work, she paved the way for leading Black scholars to provide recommendations and findings that would improve education for people of African ancestry. She is beloved and highly respected both in academia and in the African-centered community outside education. Ladson-Billings (2005) referred to Joyce King as embodying the essence of the African Yoruba Deity, Yemaja. She respectfully honored her dear friend and colleague by saying:

> One of the Orishas is a female named Yemaja. She is considered the Mother of the Orishas and of all humankind. She is regarded as a life giver, whose compassion was a healing force rescuing the faithful from all trouble. (p. 26)

To many, this captures Dr. Joyce King's spirit—a *nana*, a life giver and a healing force for the African community in the United States and abroad.

Debra Watkins lovingly refers to Joyce King as her intellectual mother and her jegna—her guide and soulmate in the work toward liberation of Black children. She shared that "King is the reason that I am doing this national work. Dr. King promised me that she would never leave my side and this remains true."

For Debra Watkins, Joyce King patiently nurtured her African consciousness with book recommendations, long and engaging conversations, and strategic planning on behalf of Black children. Debra Watkins shared that Joyce King represented a like-minded warrior in the liberation of Black children, and an ally who would never be coopted and who could garner the resources for the cause. The marriage of these two brought together people from academia, educational practitioners, spiritual guides, and grassroots organizers—all members of the Black community who coalesced for the single cause.

Both Debra Watkins and Joyce King are deeply respected both inside and outside the African-centered community. Like Debra Watkins, King straddles the worlds skillfully, which is a testament to her brilliance and her "big tent" approach. By "big tent," King reminds people of African descent that they must see themselves as connected to each other and connected to our past. Wherever our children are, there is a responsibility to add a community focus and cultural consciousness to their experience. Therefore, anyone that embraces Black excellence and liberation is invited to the table to transform the lived experiences of Black youth here and abroad. As important, both Debra Watkins and Joyce King concur that praxis (thought and action) is critical to the movement toward Black liberation.

Joyce King deeply admired CAAAE's work in California, especially the Summer Institutes held for 10 years on the Stanford University campus and for two years at UCLA (see Fig. 3) as well as her other signature programs like the Dr. Frank S. Greene Scholars that Debra Watkins started in 2001. She encouraged Debra Watkins to take the organization to a national level. Initially, Debra Watkins refused, citing how challenging it had been just doing the work in California. However, the dismal experiences of Black children in U. S. schools is well-documented. For Debra Watkins, it was worth it to entertain Joyce King's desire for a national organization.

In 2012, Debra Watkins, encouraged by Joyce King, began attending the National Black Education Agenda (NBEA) online meetings. The NBEA was founded by Dr. Sam E. Anderson, a former Black Panther Party member and SNCC activist. Dr. Anderson was a native of Brooklyn, New York, and served for five years as the education director at Medgar Evers College's Center for Law and Social Justice (Black Educator, n.d). As founder of the NBEA, he gathered educators and concerned community members virtually to discuss the problems Black children face in the educational system.

Debra Watkins recalls being blown away by the virtual meetings. The meetings connected activists from across the nation. They strategized and developed a meaningful agenda for Black children with the end goal being freedom of mind, body, and spirit. The conversations were life-changing for Debra Watkins and shifted her thoughts about taking her organization to the national level.

She came to the realization that her focus on California had been too narrow. She reflected on the fact that 80% of Black students in California graduated from high school whereas in places like Detroit, Brooklyn, and Chicago, it was often 50% or lower. After leaving the meetings, she wrote in her book *Thoughts Held Hostage: A Black Teacher's Journey to Unlocking Young Minds*:

> I felt like Jonah. God was clearly calling me to do work that could positively impact millions of our children instead of the few thousands that CAAAE had touched annually. I realized that CAAAE was uniquely positioned to spearhead this work (D. Watkins, September 16, 2021)

To Joyce King's delight, Debra Watkins finally acquiesced and made the decision in 2012 to focus on a national organization. She also decided to fund the initial planning meeting in Atlanta. She remarked that after five years she capitulated. She received her first $100,000 from the Kellogg Foundation and used that money to convene a group of what she and Dr. King now calls the "Atlanta 45"—an incubator of the best minds in Black education.

The Atlanta 45 then planned the National Black Education Summit in Chicago in October 2012 and the National Black Education Congress in 2013. In retrospect, Debra Watkins cites these convenings as one of the organization's greatest accomplishments. The recommendations from the national think tanks of leaders in education across academia, school districts, and grassroots organizers continue to inform Black education and change the trajectory of many Black academics.

The Atlanta 45

Debra Watkins, Drs. King and Anderson, and a small committee of others joined forces to begin planning the first national gathering of like-minded Black educators committed to excellence for Black youth. Together the small committee identified "praxis groups" to ensure an action-oriented agenda. The initial praxis groups focused on:

- the school-to-prison pipeline
- the development of an African-centered online course
- parent engagement courses
- 1,000 African-centered schools initiative

Debra Watkins' brainchild was the 1,000 African-centered schools initiative. Her dream was to solicit funding for 100 schools per year over the course of 10 years that would become part of a national network that would receive special training, professional development, support with grant writing and minigrants for academic and holistic enrichment. She envisioned that these African-centered schools would be models of best practices for Black education.

Approximately 100 Black educators were invited to the convening in Atlanta and 45 responded to the call. Among those trailblazers in education were Kofi Lomotey, Sharroky Hollie, Chike Akua, Joyce King, and Iva Caruthers. Debra Watkins recalled that the energized group planned what became the first gathering in Chicago in October of 2012. The goal of the summit was to lay out a national agenda for Black education.

The Black Education Working Summit (2012)

In the months leading up to the summit, Debra Watkins worked with Dr. Sharroky Hollie, cofounder of the Culture and Language Academy of Success (CLAS) in Los Angeles and featured as an Institute speaker in 2008. Hollie proved to be Watkins' greatest supporter of the 1,000 African-centered schools initiative. Working with a small team, Watkins and Hollie outlined a 2-day agenda for the Black Summit in Chicago.

Debra Watkins recalls that about 200 warriors in Black education came from all over the United States and Canada to lay out a 25-year educational agenda for the liberation of Black children. She recalled that the energy was intoxicating and that the event was magical. For some, it was life-changing. Bernard Kinsey, founder of the Kinsey art collection, inspired the crowd with his remarks. He and his wife, Shirley, are best known for their philanthropic work assisting educational/cultural institutions with educating underserved youth and increasing public awareness about African American history and ancestry.

Most importantly, the initiatives of the praxis groups were implemented. For example, an online African-centered course was introduced and ran throughout and after the event. Attendees warmly received the idea of the 1,000 schools which became the rallying call at the conference. The concept began to materialize as Debra Watkins developed a leadership team to create an action plan for implementation.

Post Summit

Following the Black summit, Debra Watkins was ready to roll out her vision of 1,000 Black schools of excellence. She turned to both Dr. Hassimi Maiga, a Songhoy language expert and chief from Mali, and Joyce King for support in naming the initiative. Dr. King had suggested including the words Black and network in the title—"ABEN": A Black Education Network. Dr. Maiga shared that the acronym also has meaning in the Songhoy language. It means "the buck stops here" or "it is finished." This double entendre had special meaning for Debra Watkins as she recalled, "I loved the name because it accurately conveyed my sentiments that education for liberation should rest with our people, not others—the buck stops with us!"

With a strong track record in fundraising and lots of connections in the philanthropy world, Debra Watkins immediately set her sights on asking her donors for $1 million dollars a year for 10 years to launch ABEN and her network of schools. To her disappointment, she received no funding. She reflected, "I was naive; No one was willing to [fund] a brand new African-centered national organization."

She sunset the CAAAE brand and grew A Black Education Network (ABEN), building on the legacy of its parent organization. She set her sights on designing a fundable model that would ensure forward movement toward her goal of a national network of exemplary Black schools. Debra Watkins placed much of her attention on growing ABEN, doubling down on her distinct philosophy with an African-centered consciousness and the long-term goal of actualizing 1,000 African-centered schools.

Her priorities were clear:

- promoting and achieving Black academic and cultural excellence in communities across the country
- networking and developing social capital for the Black community (socially, economically, and politically)
- facilitating civic action and cultural narrative change

Her mission was expansive and her target was the replication of excellent programming and coalition-building on a national scale. To do this, she needed to maximize fundraising while developing an operational structure congruent to the mission. Her first order of business postsummit was to pull together members for her Board of Directors, knowing that funders paid close attention to the board composition.

Board development

Bernard Kinsey, founder of the Kinsey Collection, agreed to serve as chairman for the inaugural board. She also solicited Paul Griffin to serve as vice chair. Years earlier, Griffin sponsored the initial CAAAE launch when he held the title of director of urban affairs for the western region of Houghton Mifflin. An avid supporter of CAAAE, he agreed to serve. Jillian Hishaw and Star Spencer, two brilliant attorneys, soon joined the ranks. Searching for someone with financial expertise, Debra Watkins sought out the services of her CAAAE accountant for the role. Michael Steele graciously accepted. She completed her board with a colleague and longtime friend, Ethiopian-born Dr. Worku Negash. His presence was invaluable as an international resource.

The Wisdom Circle

An elite group of educational phenoms, many who were former Institute keynote speakers, was selected to comprise ABEN's Wisdom Circle. This circle included educators who have been at the forefront of Black education research and innovative practices. The list of elders included endowed chairs, former AERA presidents, psychologists, grassroots organizers, and other trailblazers in the African American community.

The roster included:

- Lisa Delpit, EdD, Felton G. Clark Distinguished Professor of Education, Southern University;
- Gloria Ladson-Billings, PhD, Kellner Family Chair in Urban Education, University of Wisconsin-Madison;
- Carol Lee, PhD, Edwina S. Tarry Professor of Education & Social Policy, Northwestern University;
- Wade Nobles, PhD, Founder & Executive Director, Institute for The Advanced Study of Black Family Life and Culture;
- Adelaide Sanford, PhD, Vice Chancellor Emerita, New York Board of Regents;
- Malik Yakini, Founder & Executive Director, The Detroit Black Community Food Security Network and the Nsoroma Institute

Inducted in 2013, the Wisdom Circle were considered thought partners and avid supporters of ABEN. Debra Watkins proudly said:

> I wanted Gloria Ladson-Billings to be at the Institute last year, so I just texted her and she said yes. Basically, if there's anything that I need from them, they're just there . . . like Wade Nobles. I wanted him to come and be the keynote speaker for the Black Students of California United. Wade was the first chair of an Africana studies department in the United States. He was there (D. Watkins, personal communication, April 1, 2021).

Next, Debra Watkins focused her attention on garnering seed money for ABEN. She wanted a paid staff and guaranteed income to ensure forward traction of the organization. With a professionally designed brochure in hand, beautifully crafted to highlight the core values, mission, vision, and key stakeholders, Debra Watkins began to shop ABEN to various funders.

In a blog, Watkins wrote about her experience soliciting what would become one of ABEN's greatest supporters. She shared that as she was strategizing on ways to garner money for the new organization, she stumbled upon a blog written by Larry Kramer, the newly appointed president of the Hewlett Foundation and former dean of Stanford University's Law School. Kramer was seeking feedback from his constituents. At the time, he wanted the readers to candidly share their views about the Hewlett Foundation's philanthropy. Watkins, who remains on the pulse of the philanthropy world, immediately responded and candidly stated "that he did not want to know what my organization thought of Hewlett's giving."

To her surprise, Kramer promptly asked for her to share more. She stated that the Hewlett Foundation had a horrible track record of funding organizations led by people of color. She immediately pointed him to an article written by the Greenlining Institute that shed light on the failure of philanthropists to support communities of color. In fact, Greenlining estimated that communities of color receive less than 5% of all charitable donations from the more than 72,000 foundations in the country (Atkins & Aguilar, 2012). She added that she would be happy to meet with him to discuss "the color of philanthropy" on two conditions: 1. He must provide feedback on her new organization, ABEN, and their brochure; 2. She wanted an introduction to the recently appointed Darren Walker, African American president of the Ford Foundation. Unbeknownst to Kramer, Debra Watkins wanted the funding for the 1,000 Black schools' initiative and had targeted the Ford Foundation as the sponsor.

Debra Watkins was excited when she and Kramer met three weeks later in December, 2013. It was the beginning of a fruitful relationship that continues to this day. By the end of the conversation, ABEN was seeded $150,000 for three years, and Kramer connected her to Walker. Within three months, Debra Watkins found herself in Manhattan meeting at the offices of the Ford Foundation. Impressed by the CAAAE's work in California, Walker granted her $100,000 toward the cause. He did not fund the 1,000 Black School initiative, but they came to develop a strong and meaningful relationship.

A Black Education Congress in Chicago

While Debra Watkins continued to birth ABEN, she and Joyce King, along with Iva Carruthers, who is best known for her work in addressing social issues for people of African descent, planned a follow up to the Summit to finish their work on the 25-year education for liberation Black agenda. They met at the Westin in Chicago for what they called "The Black Education Congress." The convening attracted 150 freedom fighters to develop a 25-year education for liberation action plan. Debra Watkins recollected that Dr. King, in her brilliance, put the event together and it showed. The purpose of the praxis teams, the process that they were to follow in their praxis groups and the protocol handbook.

The praxis handbook developed for the Black Congress presented the 25-year vision of a network of Black educators and activists in the United States, Canada, and the Caribbean. Its purpose was to affirm the imperative and efficacy of models of academic and cultural excellence that serve the community. As the handbook (n.d) stated:

> Our intention is to give explicit attention to intergenerational and Pan-African collaboration—to elevate and celebrate "what works" for the education and socialization of African children, and to "pass the torch" to those coming on behind us. It is also our intention to focus on our children's education and socialization needs wherever they are—in public, private, charter, faith-based, home schools, and those out-of-school. (A Black Education Congress p. 3)

A step-by-step process was articulated including the identification of exemplary models and the identification of delegates who were charged with implementing plans in their spheres of influence after they adjourned. Delegates would choose one praxis team for their work. Praxis teams had grown to include:

- programming for the youth delegates in action (high school, post high school, and college students)
- higher education to educate students of African ancestry for academic and cultural excellence for the new millennium (graduate students and teachers)
- breaking the school-to-prison pipeline and stemming the social obscenity of mass incarceration
- identifying/implementing culturally connected teaching, learning, curriculum, and assessment
- parent leaders on elevating engagement through parent-identified best engagement practices
- 1,000 schools: creating/certifying a network of 1,000 African-centered schools (meets with the "parent leaders" praxis team)
- resilience and resistance—standing our ground on our own cultural terms

One professor and co-curriculum writer for the online course shared that participation in the Congress transformed her professional identity and research agenda. She was impressed by the Congress because she had never seen such a large group of elders collectively focused on Black education and Black traditions. As a result, the Congress motivated her to think about what she does, how she does it, and what traditions were informing her research and teaching.

From the Congress, ABEN formulated delegates who were charged with holding strategic forums around the country in the major regions including the Midwest (Detroit), the East Coast (Philadelphia), the South (Atlanta), and the West (Los Angeles). Debra Watkins wanted delegates to find allies who would join the ranks; ABEN donated $5000 to each region so that costs for each newly recruited attendee would be approximately $25.

Regional meetings began soon after the Congress. Debra Watkins heard over and over from participants that the regional meetings quenched their thirst for knowledge and collaboration. One participant from the Philadelphia forum called Debra Watkins following his session to share how energized his team was from their meeting. After speaking to her, he excitedly responded "We are the water carriers!" This soon became the ABEN tagline.

Despite all the Black convenings, Debra Watkins wistfully observed that ABEN was the only praxis group that took on the charge of the Black Congress. Disappointed and yet energized, she shared that no one else at the Congress was able to take any of their praxis ideas and implement them fully primarily because they did not have ready access to funding.

ABEN is Launched

ABEN was unlike any other "professional development" or networking organization in education at its time. The organization was grounded in holistic perspectives that honored mind, body, and spirit as well as the historic legacy of communities of African descent. With extreme clarity around the status of Black children in the United States, ABEN was born "woke." As Watkins explained while being interviewed for a Facebook live, racism has never gone asleep . . . it is alive and well and bolstered by state-sanctioned violence. Black people have been the subjects of White terrorism for 400 years. Of course, we have White allies, but at the end of the day, the allies need to show up in ways to defeat White domination and terrorism.

Carefully articulated systems and replication models, grounded in African-centered principles, culturally responsive curriculum and the upliftment of teachers of African ancestry, underscored the mission. In the final analysis, ABEN worked diligently toward its mission of reversing the backward slide of Black children in schools. Its goals were expansive—cross cutting and inclusive of health, housing, education, policy and most importantly activism, in all spheres of life in the Black community.

At its foundation was an African-centered framework. The seven core principles of the Nguzo Saba embody all aspects of ABEN's work:

- Umoja: Unity of Africa and diaspora
- Kujichagulia: Self-Determination
- Ujima: Collective work and responsibility
- Ujamaa: Cooperative economics
- Nia: Purpose
- Kuumba: Creativity

The heartbeat of the organization is represented by the final principle Faith. Spirituality permeates every action, behavior, and decision made by its board and its practitioners.

The content, aim, and method of ABEN disrupted commonly held notions of what education, reaching, teaching, and learning looked like for Black children. Over the next two decades, ABEN would put in place a model to actualize its mission through intentional fundraising, programming, and coalition-building.

To ABEN, Black excellence is ubiquitous to the organization's functions. One of the most important goals of ABEN became highlighting best practices in Black education and making those practices accessible to the masses, including holding local, state, and national stakeholders accountable to the needs of Black students, families, and communities.

Restoration of the Black community meant transforming the internal community and external public narratives about African American/Black people, histories, and achievements. The opportunity gaps between Black and White students represented one of the greatest problems that needed to be addressed. In its place, ABEN sought to focus on promoting the legacy of excellence in academic achievement as a historical and cultural core value among and goal for African American/Black students.

ABEN Programming

ABEN became the umbrella organization for several institutions founded by Debra Watkins. ABEN was continuing the work of CAAAE as a direct support for Black Students moving through the K-16 pipeline. Debra Watkins proudly boasts that of most import to her work is centering Black children. She emphatically states "you will never see a stock image on her website. Those beautiful children are our scholars. We always center the children."

ABEN began implementing cultural enrichment programs and services on the national level in the form of after school and Saturday programming in both school and nonschool settings. Each of these programs was designed to foster cultural and historic pride and to engage parents and other family members. In 2016, after CAAAE's name was sunset and it became ABEN, two institutions that had been founded by Debra Watkins were spun off as their own independent nonprofits.

The Dr. Frank S. Greene Scholars Program

Debra Watkins is most proud of the Greene Scholars program (GSP), a STEM Program established in 2001 for Black children in Silicon Valley. STEM is especially dear to Debra Watkins' heart because it demonstrates the intergenerational brilliance of African scientific innovation from the past to the present. Like many who came before (Ben-Jochannan, 1988; Diop, 1974; Williams, 1971) she recognized that Africans were the first humans and they developed the oldest documented civilization. Pioneers of science, technology, engineering, and math, Africans built the pyramids of the Gaza plains, the Nubian temples, and the great obelisks of Axum. They also developed mathematical calculations on the Ishango bone. In the 15th century, the classic sculptures of the Benin bronzes demonstrated the knowledge of how to cast in brass and bronze. The great stone temples of Zimbabwe demonstrated advanced stone masonry, all representing forms of ingenuity in art, masonry, engineering, and other areas (Koutonin, 2016).

Debra Watkins finds it a travesty that children of African ancestry may not know their historic legacy and the power within their DNA, especially as it relates to STEM. GSP provides long-term youth development support for Black students from Grades 3 through 12. Programming includes hands-on math, science, and technology experiences and workshops; science fairs and engineering competitions; and entrepreneurial/leadership programs.

The program was named after Dr. Frank S. Greene, a scientist and venture capitalist, who worked in the Bay Area of California. He is remembered as a dedicated and caring jegna and teacher, and an inspirational role model. Considered one of the pioneers of semiconductor technology, Greene paved the way for Black engineers as he helped break the color barrier in Silicon Valley.

Greene scholars boast an impressive success rate. One hundred percent of its scholars go to college, 90% graduate in 4 years with BA or BS degrees, and 60% of them earn degrees in STEM fields (Watkins, 2016). One Greene Scholar shared, "The Greene Scholars Program has grounded me in a community of peers and jegna that have exemplified, encouraged, and inspired academic excellence and social responsibility" (A. Olukotun, personal communication, October 4, 2023).

Black Students of California United

In the spring of 2016, Angie Barfield, Jacky McFadden, Debra Watkins, and Dr. Angelo Williams founded the Black Students of California United (BSCU). BSCU is a statewide organization focused on developing Black students through leadership training, civic engagement, project-based learning, and dual generational engagement.

Webinars and Other Programming

Another priority of ABEN became designing networking opportunities for its participants to connect with each other, to share culturally responsive resources, to develop leadership skills, and to mobilize. Like its mother organization CAAAE, ABEN continued the legacy of organizing and hosting meetings and Institutes. ABEN expanded to include webinars, and cultural education activities designed to enable educators to integrate culturally appropriate strategies both to better teach African American students and to close academic opportunity gaps. In 2021, ABEN offered webinars such as Curriculum Trauma, Deconstructing the Impact of White Supremacy in American Education; Antiracist Discipline; Changing the Narrative: Trauma Responsive Schools and Classroom; and Digital Diversity with Brian Brown. Its public Facebook page holds enriching resources to support best practice in Black education and to highlight a more accurate storytelling of the history of Africans in the diaspora.

In addition to the institutes, ABEN is also noted for its outstanding professional development offerings and African-centered after-school programs.

The ABEN Summer Institutes

In 2016, after a 4-year hiatus, ABEN reintroduced its highly acclaimed Summer Institutes held at Stanford University. Professor Dr. Arnetha Ball, director of the Center for Race, Ethnicity, and Language at Stanford, was the keynote speaker in 2016. In 2017, Stephen D. Hancock, PhD and Associate Professor of Multicultural Education in the Department of Reading and Elementary Education, was the keynote speaker. In 2019, Dr. Beverly Daniel Tatum was featured, marking her second keynote at the ABEN Institute in honor of the

20th anniversary of her seminal book entitled *Why Are All the Black Kids Sitting Together in the Cafeteria and Other Conversations About Race.*

Because ABEN had so much success with the regional conferences, Debra Watkins decided to take her more popular speakers on the road because they were so well received at the Institute. She also recognized that not everyone could attend. In all, there were five speakers—Anthony Browder, Chike Akua, Kobie Wilkerson, Stephen Hancock, and Hashim Jabar. They were met with sold-out crowds in many of the venues in Philadelphia, Chicago, and Atlanta.

When COVID-19 and anti-Black racism came to a head in 2020, ABEN reset. The ABEN Institutes went virtual, providing access to educators and community organizers across the nation and abroad. In 2020, the 15th Annual Virtual Summer Institute sold out. With educational giants such as Iva Carruthers, Linda Darling-Hammond, Joyce King, and Gloria Ladson-Billings gracing the virtual Zoom screen, the three-day Institute was a huge success.

In 2021, Bettina Love was invited to keynote. She brought the fire as she addressed the plight of Black students in California. The audience was graced with elders Joyce King and Iva Carruthers as respondents as they provided context and situated the young scholars' work within an African-centered

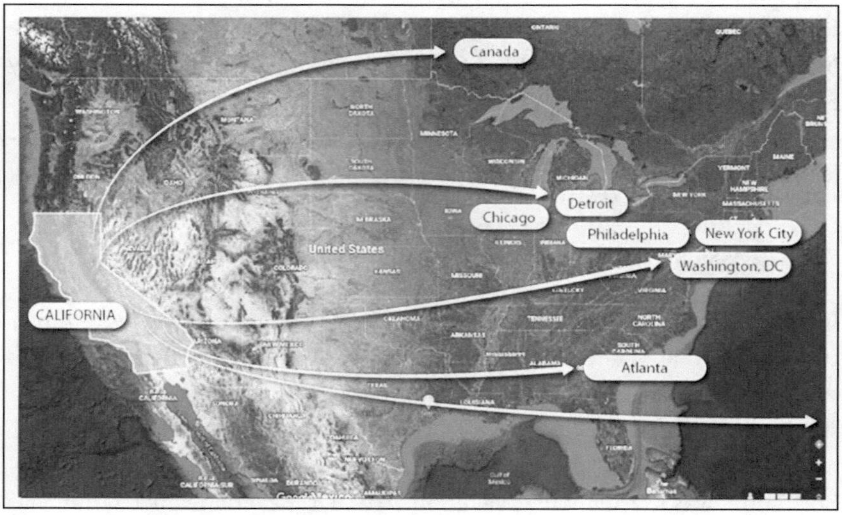

Figure 2.4. ABEN 2014–2019 — The ABEN Road Tour.

context. Participants shared that they loved the resource recommendations and they deeply appreciated the time to plan an action with their districts.

One participant stated that her favorite part was being around insightful, funny, charismatic, passionate, and creative people and minds! Another enjoyed most being part of a community that affirms the things that she had begun to think about in her spirit but in some cases didn't have the language, experience, or knowledge to articulate. New information, perspectives, resources! Even virtually, like other ABEN Institutes, the convening served as "the watering hole" and its players became "the water carriers."

Civic Action

Political action and advocacy became the final hallmark of the organization. Recognizing that ABEN works both within and outside of the African American community, it moved toward providing mechanisms for collective action in the policy realm. ABEN embraced *participatory action research*, which holds the belief that those who are most impacted by research should be the ones taking the lead in framing the questions, the design, methods, and the modes of analysis of such research projects. Likewise, ABEN leaned on engaging in policy analysis activities that examined the impacts of current and historic public policies on African American/Black academic and cultural achievement. ABEN supports its members by developing and implementing policy recommendations across the nation.

Global Reach: Virtual Trips to Ghana and Nigeria

ABEN took full advantage of the virtual realm to grow its network internationally. In 2000, Debra Watkins traveled to Ghana and the trip was life-changing. During COVID-19, she decided to make that experience a reality for school children by sponsoring and hosting two virtual trips to Ghana. Debra Watkins believes that children need to see what Africa is like as a way to love being African. A total of 330 children and chaperones participated. On its second journey, ABEN left a significant contribution to the Thread Foundation, an organization dedicated to improving the lives of Ghanaian children. The journey was captured in Debra Watkins' and Monica

Utsey's *WE DID THAT!: Traveling to Ghana During the 2020 Pandemic*, which became an Amazon best seller. The following year, ABEN expanded its tours to include a virtual trip to Nigeria and has plans for a virtual trip to Kenya in the near future.

ABEN Looks Forward

Through the intentional leadership and philanthropic efforts of ABEN's founder, Debra Watkins, ABEN has grown from a small, volunteer-based organization to a multitiered system that connects Black students, teachers, families, organizers, school districts, politicians, academics, churches, and other stakeholders in the community.

Today, the board and its players remain all Black and its organization has garnered millions of dollars to support the mission. Over the years, Debra Watkins has remained focused. She never forgets that communities of African ancestry are at war. Paying close attention to the past, she recognizes that she stands on the legacy of her ancestors. Debra Watkins walks in purpose and owns her calling. Building more allies and positioning herself for funding, ABEN is poised to move toward the goal of 1,000 African-centered schools. In 2021 alone, over 1,822 Black children and families were positively impacted by its programming and the numbers are growing.

The next chapters highlight voices from within the ABEN community. Each will speak to the impact that the organization has had on their personal and professional growth. Part II delves into the soul-centered leadership of Debra Watkins, her backstory, and her drivers. Part II is followed by those individuals deeply impacted by Debra Watkins' leadership and support.

Questions

What is the history of your organization? What professional development resources do you use for fundraising and program evaluation to support the growth and development of your work?

References

ABEN: A Black Education Network (n.d.) Home [Facebook page]. Facebook. Retrieved January 15, 2022, from https://www.facebook.com/ABEN4ACE/videos/420432109381045.

Atkins, A., & Aguilar, O. (2012). *A promise to diverse communities: Summary of foundation coalition's efforts*. The Greenlining Institute.

Ben-Jochannan, Y. (1988). *Africa: Mother of Western civilization*. Black Classic Press.

Black Educator. (n.d). A brief bio of S. E. Anderson. *Black Education for Liberation*. https://www.blackeducator.org/

Diop, C. A. (1974). *The African origin of civilization: Myth or reality* (M. Cook, Ed. & Trans.). Lawrence Hill Books. (Original works published 1954 and 1967)

King, J. E. (Ed.). (2005). *Black education: A transformative research and action agenda for the new century*. Routledge.

Koutonin, M. (2016). *Lost cities #9: Racism and ruins—the plundering of Great Zimbabwe*. https://www.theguardian.com/cities/2016/aug/18/great-zimbabwe-medieval-lost-city-racism-ruins-plundering

Ladson-Billings, G. (2005). *Beyond the big house: African American educators on teacher education*. Teacher College Press.

National Alliance for Black School Educators. (n.d.). *Our history*. NABSE. https://www.nabse.org/about/our-history/

Tatum, B.D. (1997). *Why are all the Black kids sitting together in the cafeteria and other conversations about race*. Basic Books.

Watkins, D. (2016). *Thoughts held hostage: A Black teacher's journey to unlocking young minds*. A Black Education Network.

Williams, C. (1971). *The destruction of Black civilization: Great issues of a race from 4500 B.C. to 2000 A.D.* Third World Press.

PART II

SOUL-CENTERED PROGRAMMING

THREE

The Cultural Imperative Initiative

Anthony T. Browder

> An act does not end at the end of its occurrence. It continues moving down through the ages, influencing generation, after generation, after generation.
>
> —*Dr. Amos Wilson*

TO UNDERSTAND THE PIVOTAL ROLE A Black Education Network (ABEN) has played in my work with students since 2014, it is important to give a broad context that leads up to that engagement. Education is as important to a person's mental, physical, and spiritual development as is the air they breathe. An ideal education not only benefits individuals but also the communities in which individuals live, ensuring harmony within that community for generations. In traditional African societies, educational norms were established to ensure group unity and identity. Culture was the glue that held communities together. Culture is ordered behavior, and cultural imperatives were established by elders within a community to ensure that every person understood their responsibility to help maintain order within the collective.

The idea of a cultural imperative was best expressed by the word *ubuntu* among the Zulu and Xhosa of South Africa. Ubuntu embodies the humanitarian bonds that link everyone in the community to the collective. A simple translation of ubuntu is: "I am because we are and we are because I am." Ubuntu represents the simple reality within a community that "a person is a person because there are people."

The bonds of communal engagement that sustained Africans for thousands of generations were broken during the *Maafa*—the great disaster that is often referred to as slavery. In order to maintain this oppressive system, Europeans had to miseducate enslaved Africans and force them to accept the lie that they had no culture in Africa, and that embracing European values was their only means of survival in a cruel New World.

The current conditions of dysfunction, violence, and economic deprivation that we find in Black communities throughout America are a direct result of 400 years of miseducation and abuse. The only viable means of reversing these conditions is by implementing new methods to reeducate and resocialize

Black people because whoever controls the education of Black people controls their destiny and the destinies of the communities in which they live.

The importance of education to people of African descent was exemplified by two African American educators in the early 20th century, Arthur Schomburg and John Henrik Clarke. Schomburg wrote that

> The American Negro must remake his past in order to make his future. What is a luxury for the nation as a whole becomes a prime social necessity for the Negro. For him, a group tradition must supply compensation for persecution, and pride of race the antidote for prejudice. History must restore what slavery took away, for it is the social damage of slavery that the present generation must repair and offset. So among the rising democratic millions we find the Negro thinking more collectively, more retrospectively than the rest, and apt out of the very pressure of the present to become the most enthusiastic antiquarian of them all. (Shomburg, 1926)

Schomburg's words inspired a young man from Union Springs, Alabama, named John Henrik Clarke, who traveled to Harlem in 1933 to seek advice from Schomburg on how he could better his education. The young, brash 18-year-old asked Schomburg to teach him all he knew about the history of African people. Unamused, the 59-year-old Schomburg told Clarke, "What you're calling African history and Negro history are the missing pages of world history . . . son, go and study your master. Go study the history of the people who enslaved you and find out why they found it a necessity to remove an entire people from the respectable commentary of the history of the world."

The young Clarke took Schomburg's advice and gained a wealth of knowledge about European history and world history. When Clarke returned to Mr. Schomburg, armed with knowledge to better appreciate the wisdom Schomburg possessed, he taught Clarke the interrelationship of African history to world history and geographical reference and its capacity to awaken the historical consciousness of a people.

After Schomburg's death in 1938, Clarke's intellectual development was further nurtured by his relationships with Willis N. Huggins, John G. Jackson, and William Leo Hansberry. These men were among the foremost intellectuals in Harlem during the 1940s, and under their tutelage, Clarke went on to become one of the most important educators and intellectuals in the late 20th

century. Clarke was also associated with some of the most important historical organizations in the country. For example, Clarke was vice president for the Association for the Study of Negro Life and History from 1949–1955; hosted the first meeting of the Organization of Afro-American Unity at his Harlem home with Malcolm X in 1965; was the founding president of the African Heritage Studies Association in 1969; and was a founding member of the Association for the Study of Classical African Civilization in 1984.

Dr. Clarke spent his most productive years as a classroom teacher instructing generations of students, many of whom went on to become educators in high schools and colleges throughout the United States and Africa. Dr. Clarke's passion as an educator instilled within his students a burning desire to embrace a cultural imperative that ignited within them the passion to liberate the minds of African people and free the African spirit that laid dormant within them. This indomitable spirit had been suppressed for centuries, patiently awaiting the opportunity to reemerge and reunite with other liberated souls to recreate a world by and for people of African descent.

This desire was ignited within me upon meeting Dr. Clarke in 1981. This initial meeting set in motion events that would lead to piloting a Cultural Imperative Initiative (CII) in three high schools in San Jose, CA over three decades later. Three years of fine tuning the CII in California evolved into the creation of cultural imperative programs (CIP) offered in classrooms and community centers throughout the United States beginning in 2018. The undeniable influence of Dr. John Henrik Clarke's and Dr. Asa G. Hilliard's teachings on the development of the two cultural imperative projects is worth sharing for those wishing to establish similar programs in their schools and communities.

As a child born in Chicago, IL in 1951, I grew up in an era before teaching Black History was popular. While youth of my generation were not taught Black History in school, we were taught to adhere to three basic directives in our communities:

1) Respect your elders.
2) Be a credit to your race.
3) Strive to get as much education as possible.

Respect Your Elders and be a Credit to Your Race

Most Black folk living in the North in the 1950s were the offspring of parents or grandparents who participated in the Great Migration from the Southern states of Alabama, Mississippi, Georgia, North and South Carolina, and Florida into the Northern urban ghettos in Chicago, Detroit, Philadelphia, and New York City. Between 1940 and 1970, more than four million Black families fled the segregated South seeking freedom, justice, and equality in the North.

Upon arrival in the North, Blacks were huddled into pockets of poverty created by redlining and restrictive covenants that were overseen by racist politicians, bankers, real estate agents, and attorneys. Southern Black families arrived up North holding on to honored traditions that were shared with their families. Children often lived in the same house or apartment with their parents, grandparents, aunts, and uncles. Within these households, youth were taught to respect their parents and every elder in the community. Without being fully aware of the African retentions at play, Black communities were living out the Ghanaian maxim: "It takes one woman to have a child, but it takes a village to raise it." Every apartment building and home, every block in every neighborhood, was a village where every adult was responsible for the well-being of every child in their village, whether they were related to them or not.

The upside of living in segregated communities, in a racist city and country, was that Black people knew they were dependent on each other for their collective survival. People looked out for each other because they knew that they were all they had. They could not depend on politicians or police because the racial restrictions in America always reminded them that they were second class citizens. The one redeeming quality was that the Southern traditions carried into Northern environments encouraged family cohesion and respect for elders in the household and the community. Of equal or greater importance was the expectation that every man, woman, and child conduct themselves in a manner that would not bring shame to their family, community, or race. The actions of one person in the community/village were a reflection on everyone living in the community/village. Everyone celebrated the success of one person and grieved the missteps of another.

Marcus Garvey, founder of the Universal Negro Improvement Association (UNIA), popularized the idea of being a race man or race woman. Garvey immigrated from Jamaica to Harlem in 1916 and tapped into the cultural zeitgeist of millions of blacks in America who understood the importance of "uplifting the race" and not bringing shame on their family, community, or race. Garvey's UNIA was the largest Black-led cultural organization in the world. In addition to stressing Black pride and cooperative economics, Garvey also stressed the importance of history and education as essential elements in reshaping the minds of a population that had been written out of the respectable commentary of human history.

Throughout our long sojourn in the Americas, Black folk were socialized to believe that a good education was the best way to ensure economic security, and respect and admiration from one's family and community. These teachings were constantly impressed upon Black children early in life and reinforced in school and church, in the home, and on the playground. Additionally, young Black children saw numerous examples of Black pride and excellence in their communities. Doctors, lawyers, teachers, preachers, postal workers, and street sweepers all took pride in their work and were a source of inspiration for young and old. People were encouraged to excel and do good for the pride that it would bring to their family, their community, and their race.

From the 1930s through the 1960s, Blacks were encouraged to be intelligent and articulate as a means of fighting back against racism and uplifting the race. Education was one of the most accessible ways of uplifting individuals and the race during times when the fallacy of "separate but equal" was the law of the land. Teaching was viewed as an honorable profession and was one of the few job opportunities open to Black people in America.

During the days of segregated schools, many Black children were taught by Black teachers who had a vested interest in their student's education. Black teachers often attended the same churches as their students and their parents. They often lived in the same neighborhoods and patronized the same beauty shops and barbers, shopped in the same stores, and belonged to the same social organizations.

Living in this type of cultural incubator instilled a sense of cohesiveness within the community, which, in effect, turned segregated communities into sacred spaces where everyone had a vested interest in the well-being of all the children in the community. There was even a code of ethics among the criminal element within the Black community. Drugs were not sold to children, and one would not think about stealing from an elder.

During the 13 years of the Civil Rights Movement (which was bookended by the murder of 14-year-old Emmet Till in 1955 and the assassination of 39-year-old Dr. Martin Luther King, Jr. in 1968), some Blacks were actively involved in a reeducation process that recalibrated the consciousness of a critical mass who were mentally evolving from Colored to Negro to Black and proud! Many of these newly conscious Blacks were high school and college students who were frustrated by the apparent shortcoming of the Civil Rights Movement and sought methods that would bring about more immediate changes in their lives.

As more Black students pursued higher education in the 1960s, we witnessed growing protests from students who demanded Black Studies courses in their colleges and universities. They enrolled in Black Studies courses, and desired to learn more about ancient African history and current events in the motherland. These changes in consciousness were reflected in new fashion trends, which swept across the country and began influencing young people worldwide. Young Blacks began wearing Afros, African clothing and jewelry, and taking on African names. Young Blacks in America and the Caribbean were also inspired by African leaders who were shaking off the bonds of colonialism by liberating the minds of their citizens and their nations.

Kwame Nkrumah acknowledged that he was radicalized while studying at Lincoln University in Pennsylvania and his frequent trips to Harlem where he interacted with John Henrik Clarke and other Black intellectuals. In 1957, Nkrumah became the first president of the former British colony known as the Gold Coast and he promptly renamed the country Ghana. Nkrumah also invited his friend John Clarke to work in his administration.

The Nigerian multi-instrumentalist and political activist Fela Kuti spent 10 months in Los Angeles in 1969, where he discovered the Black Power Movement, the music of James Brown, and R&B. Fela often said that he had to come to America to learn African history and the beauty of his African heritage. Stephen Biko, the South African anti-apartheid activist, was similarly influenced by the Black Power Movement in the United States. Biko became the leader of the Black Consciousness Movement during the late 60s and 70s before he was brutally murdered in 1977 while in police custody.

An honest assessment of the 1960s will show that it was one of the most violent decades in U.S. history. The world witnessed the killings of Medgar Evers, Malcolm X, Martin Luther King, and scores of Civil Rights activists.

Television cameras broadcast images of church bombings in Birmingham, the brutal beatings of protestors in Selma, and attacks on innocent student protestors. Despite all of this sadness and grief, or maybe because of it, the 1960s was also a decade in which thousands of young, gifted, and Black folk changed the course of U.S. history and, ultimately, the course of world history.

People of African descent around the world were beginning to realize that the White racist system that had controlled their lives and the lives of their ancestors for hundreds of years, could no longer control a culturally conscious people who were willing to fight and die for their freedom. But in a world governed by immutable laws, one law held sway: "Newton's Third Law," which stipulated that "for every action, there is an equal and opposite reaction." The foreshadowed reaction was that racist nations would not sit idly by and allow oppressed Black folk throughout the world to free themselves. Racist Europeans understood that the systems of slavery, colonization, segregation, Jim Crow, and apartheid which they created for their own genetic survival, must be maintained if Whites were to continue to control the planet and all its resources.

The counteroffensive was brutal in Africa as the American CIA worked with European Intelligence offices to assassinate African leaders and overthrow democratically elected governments. The counteroffensive was more subtle in the United States but equally destructive. Recently released COINTELPRO documents revealed that there were a series of covert and illegal operations conducted by the FBI between 1956 and 1971, to surveil, infiltrate, discredit, and disrupt Black social and political organizations. Some Black leaders were killed, and many others became political prisoners and spent decades in prison.

A critical assessment of U.S. history between the 1960s and 1980s shows the willful destruction of Black communities that were being transformed by the cultivation of a new Black consciousness focused on the restoration of African historical and cultural values. The destruction took the form of dismantling Black communities and the educational and cultural institutions that sustained them by introducing welfare legislation designed to destroy traditional family structures and values. The final twin pillars of destruction were the proliferation of drugs that destroyed minds and bodies, and the introduction of new forms of music that glorified drugs, violence, and misogyny. Music that once encouraged folk to be Black and proud now encouraged them to kill each other and disrespect the women in their communities. Black youth who strove to be intelligent and articulate in the 1960s were socialized in the 1980s to believe that to be smart and articulate was acting White. Ideals of collective racial pride gave way to the selfish pursuit of material gains. Respect for elders, women, children, and the community were now considered relics of a bygone era dominated by young men who terrorized their own neighbors. The long-term effects of such behaviors are well documented in Michelle Alexander's book, *The New Jim Crow: Mass Incarceration in the Age of Colorblindness*, and Ava DuVernay's documentary, *The 13th*.

In hindsight, the long-term effects of Civil Rights legislation passed in the 1960s resulted in the disintegration and destruction of Black communities like Bronzeville in Chicago and Harlem in New York City. Whether this was the intent or not will be debated by sociologists and political scientists for generations. But the outcomes speak for themselves. The demise of insular Black communities in segregated America resulted in the collapse of social safety nets that ensured the success of Black families, especially Black children who were no longer being taught by Black teachers who had a vested interest in their success and emotional well-being.

Prior to the establishment of Negro History Week in 1926, and its expansion into Black History Month in 1977, school-aged Black youth were taught very little about "Negro history." In the early 20th century, most textbooks taught that Negroes (Africans) had no history, culture, religion, or civilization prior to their enslavement. Most history books propagated the myth that Africans lived in darkness until Europeans brought them into the light. Generations of Black folk (Africans and Negroes) were miseducated to believe lies that were reinforced within school systems created and funded by people of European ancestry. This injustice was backed up by the full weight of local, state, and national legislation put in place as early as 1619 and it continues into the present day.

Evolution of Cultural Imperative Initiatives

The creation of organizations and movements (eg., The Association for the Study of Negro Life and History, NAACP, UNIA, New Negro Movement, Nation of Islam, Black Panther Party, Black Consciousness Movement) represented efforts among Black leadership to implement and maintain cultural imperatives to validate the humanity of people of African descent and ensure that their stories are properly told.

The value of Arthur Schomburg's article, "The Negro digs up his past," becomes apparent to any person who followed Schomburg's advice and did a little digging themselves. Even a superficial investigation into Negro history reveals evidence of "forbidden knowledge" hidden in books written by people of African ancestry. Many of these books documented a historical narrative, replete with scientific and archeological evidence that proved that Africa was the birthplace of humanity, culture, and civilization.

The challenge facing anyone whose life has been transformed by exposure to such forbidden knowledge is "How do we get this empowering information to the masses of Black folk who have been denied access to these transformative historical truths?" One must also be aware of similar efforts in the past to share this knowledge and the push back by some of the very people whose lives have been adversely impacted by the absence of this knowledge and whose lives could be transformed by it.

Unfortunately, many have held on to the unreasonable belief that those who created and profited from systems that justified kidnapping; enslavement; physical, emotional, and sexual abuse; and murder would confess their sins, beg for forgiveness, and implement steps to ensure forms of reparative justice. The only appropriate response to continual injustices is for the victims to make mental declarations of independence from their abusers and begin processes of healing and self-repair. This is best accomplished by enacting cultural imperative initiatives.

A cultural imperative initiative addresses the needs of self-determined people to define the actions that will ensure the preservation of social behaviors, knowledge, beliefs, laws, customs, and traditions thus guaranteeing their capacity to grow and thrive for generations.

Cultural imperative initiatives are not new; they have been implemented in some form or another wherever people have lived. In traditional African societies, cultural imperative initiatives were ritualized in all aspects of life and connected the unborn, the living, and the ancestors through a series of rituals that bound them together as one living entity. The social structures that thrived in Africa for thousands of years were disrupted during the Arab and European enslavement of Africans and entire communities were decimated. Although the capacity to maintain cultural cohesiveness within African communities was lost during enslavement, the ability to restore it has remained locked inside the DNA of every African regardless of where they are. All that is required to access these dormant abilities is the restoration of their historical and cultural memories.

Currently, the framework for establishing and maintaining cultural imperative initiatives for disenfranchised African populations around the world consists of three basic components:

- restoration of historical memory
- restoration of cultural memory
- implementation of strategic plans to ritualize historical and cultural practices

Restoration of Historical and Cultural Memory

> History is the clock people use to tell their political and cultural time of day. History is the compass people use to find themselves on the map of human geography. History tells a people who they were and who they are. (Clarke, 1992)

The most important role of history is to tell a people where they are going and what they must do to get there.

Dr. Clarke often compared the relationship between a people and their history to that of a child and her mother. In that respect, since 1619, Blacks in America have lived as motherless children who have been continuously abused by their adoptive American parents for more than 400 years.

Multiple generations of Africans in America were subjected to constant trauma and abuse at the hands of their former enslavers and the state while living through decades of Jim Crow and segregation. Unfortunately, abuses continued over an extensive period can become normalized to the point where the abused becomes the abuser and inflicts pain and suffering on themselves and the people closest to them. Through the newly emerging science of epigenetics, we now know that the genes of people exposed to trauma are permanently altered and immediately passed on to their offspring. This fact sheds light on the saying that "hurt people, hurt people." It is because the legacy of hurt and abuse has been encoded into their DNA.

The trauma and abuse that has been inflicted upon enslaved people in the United States and their descendants has left emotional scars that are often unseen and thus more difficult to treat. In this regard, the long-term effects of mental abuse and trauma can sometimes cause more harm than physical abuse alone because after physical wounds have healed and the pain associated with them has subsided, the effects of mental abuse continue to fester. Such lingering mental health problems are now referred to as post-traumatic stress disorder (PTSD), which has been associated with war veterans, but one must also inquire about the mental well-being of the victims of war.

The late psychiatrist, Patricia Newton, MD, often commented that the Africans who got on the slave ships were not the same as the Africans who got off the slave ships. The trauma of being kidnapped, imprisoned in slave dungeons, packed in slave ships, shackled and forced to endure unimaginable abuse during the two to three-months-long journey across the ocean was enough trauma to forever alter the genes of the survivors. Once the survivors of the Middle Passage disembarked in America, they experienced new levels of trauma and abuse as they were sold, separated, and forced to endure a lifetime of labor without compensation.

Dr. Newton referred to both the survivors of such trauma and their modern descendants, as victims of *post-traumatic slave disorder* (PTSD). Although some have referred to this condition as *post-traumatic slavery syndrome*, Dr. Newton stated that there is a profound distinction between a disorder and syndrome. According to Dr. Newton, a syndrome is a set of symptoms associated with a particular disorder and a disorder is a particular abnormal condition that negatively affects the functionality of a person.

One proven means of minimizing and or reversing the lingering effects of PTSD is to introduce patients to alternative historical narratives. This creates new memories that establish new neurological pathways that rewire the brain and create a new range of internal reactions to external stimuli. This complex treatment modality can be best summed up by the statements, "Neurons that wire together fire together," and "If you knew better, you would do better."

Another African American psychiatrist, Frances Cress Welsing, MD, put this theory into practice several decades ago and favorably changed the behavior of many of her patients who were unsuspectedly victims of PTSD. Dr. Welsing suggested that her African American patients watch a weekly 30-minute television program called *For the People* that aired on Howard University's TV station. *For the People* originated in Columbia, SC on a local Public Broadcasting Station (PBS) and was shared with other PBS affiliates on the East Coast. The program was created specifically "To properly place African people in human history."

For the People was hosted by Listervelt Middleton, a native South Carolinian who grew up seldom seeing positive portrayals of Black people on local or national television. Mr. Middleton addressed these concerns by producing and hosting 30-minute interviews with local Black residents. He showcased their lives and their successes as they established meaningful careers despite living in one of the most racially oppressive states in America.

The favorable responses that Mr. Middleton and the television management received from viewers let them know that they had a hit on their hands. Mr. Middleton then proceeded to host interviews with noted historians from South Carolina who lived outside the state. His interviews with Chancellor Williams, author of *Destruction of Black Civilization* and John G. Jackson, author of *Introduction to African Civilization* were among the highest rated shows on the network.

Mr. Middleton, who was an avid reader of African history, invited his friend Asa Hilliard on the show, and the interviews they conducted changed the course of history for thousands of viewers. Dr. Asa G. Hilliard, III was an educational psychologist who also specialized in the history of ancient Egypt. Although Dr. Hilliard was not a native of South Carolina (he was actually born in Texas and lived in Atlanta, GA), through his relationship with Middleton, Hilliard impressed upon Milddleton that he should use his television program to reprogram the consciousness of his viewers.

The outcome of their conversation was the creation of 13 shows with Dr. Hilliard called, *Free Your Mind, Return to the Source* (Middleton, 1986). Over the course of thirteen 30-minute interviews, Dr. Hilliard and Mr. Middleton told the story of 200,000 years of African history beginning with documenting the African origins of humanity in East Africa, the migration of people out of Africa into Asia, and populating every land mass on Earth. Dr. Hilliard presented the latest scientific data that proved that every human being on earth could be traced through their mitochondrial DNA to the very first woman who lived in East Africa 200,000 years ago (Hilliard, 1978).

Mr. Middleton spent a considerable amount of time with Dr. Hilliard discussing the African origins of Nile Valley civilizations and ancient Egypt. During the course of his interviews, Dr. Hilliard presented 13 pieces of historical and scientific evidence to substantiate his claim that the historical record

of ancient Egypt had been falsified by European scholars. The television viewers who watched this series became increasingly excited with each episode. Nothing like this had ever been seen on television before. The people were hungry and they wanted more.

Listervelt proceeded to bring on other non-South Carolinian guests who, like Dr. Hilliard, introduced viewers to new historical narratives about the global accomplishments of people of African ancestry. Middleton featured interviews with historians, psychologists, psychiatrists, mathematicians, engineers, artists, and musicians who shared stories about African excellence, which transformed the lives of every person who watched *For the People*.

Dr. Welsing told her medical colleagues and audiences worldwide how she successfully altered the disruptive patterns of both criminal behavior and drug and alcohol abuse among many of her patients simply by having them watch episodes of *For the People* and discussing the programs in their therapy sessions. Welsing found that people who were not being treated for mental and emotional disorders also benefited from internalizing 30 minutes of positive, life-affirming programming in weekly doses.

During the 1980s, Washington, D.C. was the hub of cultural activities in the nation. It was affectionately known as "chocolate city." It had a population of over 70% Black, a Black mayor, and a predominantly Black city council. D.C. had three Black-owned radio stations that featured regular talk shows, and at least six Black newspapers. D.C. was also home to Howard University, which had its own TV and radio station.

For the People aired three days a week on Howard's TV station and helped raise the consciousness of a significant number of African Americans who lived in D.C., Maryland, and Virginia. On Memorial Day of 1987, my organization (IKG) invited Dr. Hilliard as a guest speaker for our new monthly "Free Your Mind" lecture series. The program sold out as soon as tickets were available, as did every program we sponsored over the next 5 years. The key to our success was that we booked practically every speaker who had appeared on *For the People*, including its host Listervelt Middleton.

Because many of the lecturers were educators, we invited students, teachers, and administrators to our programs. Ultimately, we were able to encourage schools to incorporate some of the content to which they had been exposed into their curriculum. Some schools even invited some of our speakers to provide in-service training to teachers in their schools.

As a result of my ongoing relationship with many of the scholars I brought to Washington, I received an education that far exceeded the one I received in school. I began sharing the knowledge I learned while sitting at the feet of some of the most brilliant minds of the late 20th century and incorporated this wisdom in my speaking engagements at schools, universities, and conferences. I also discussed history and culture in numerous radio and television interviews and in the books I wrote and published. My first book, *From the Browder File: 22 Essays on the African American Experience* became an international best-seller and the introduction was written by my dear friend Asa Hilliard. My second book, *Nile Valley Contributions to Civilization*, included an introduction by John Henrik Clarke, and it also became an international best-seller. These two publications, plus my growing reputation as an educator, public speaker, and historian, led to my invitation to speak at an ABEN Conference in October 2013.

In February 2014, I was invited by ABEN's founder, Debra Watkins, to address a group of 200 African American males at Independence High School in San Jose, CA. My talk was so enthusiastically received that Ms. Watkins asked how many of the young men would be interested in hearing Mr. Browder speak on a regular basis? From that initial meeting, I was invited to travel to San Jose monthly to speak to a group of young men who were participating in a local rites of passage program. My participation in the rites of passage training continued until the program ended a year later. As we reviewed the impact of the program, Ms. Watkins and I discussed other ways in which I could share my knowledge of history and culture in a school district with an African American population of less than 5%. I stressed the importance of including young ladies in future activities because of the urgent need to enlighten African American youth who spent their lives in a cultural desert. They were minorities in every classroom and were seldom taught any historical or cultural information that would equip them for life. These conversations inspired the creation of the Cultural Imperative Initiative.

Our plan was to select 15 to 20 African American students from three area high schools for monthly meetings where I would facilitate discussion on my book *From the Browder File*. The students wrote reflection papers on each essay and participated in discussions on their reflection papers and the essays they read.

From the Browder File was selected for the CII classes because it is an easy read and each essay is chock full of information that engaged students and expanded their understanding of African and African American history and culture. We were also aware of how transformative these sessions would be for adults, so we added a parental component to CII. This created opportunities for the entire family to engage in meaningful conversations about the *Browder File* essays at home.

Cultural Imperative Initiative Overview

The purpose of the CII is to increase cultural awareness and critical thinking skills among high school students of color. Critical thinking skills are not only essential to academic success but they also influence how students navigate their day-to-day activities. The foundation of cultural awareness is created by knowledge of historically accurate interpretations of African history and culture. This knowledge positively impacts students' self-image and behavior and strengthens their connection to African and African American people, places, and things.

The behavior and expectations of the Cultural Imperative Initiative are guided by ancient African spiritual values. All students are expected to exhibit behavior that aligns with the virtues and principles listed below:

The Seven Principles of *Maat*

1. truth
2. justice
3. righteousness
4. reciprocity
5. balance
6. order
7. harmony

The Ten Virtues

1. control of thought
2. control of action

3. steadfastness of purpose
4. identification with higher ideals
5. evidence of a mission
6. evidence of a call to spiritual order
7. freedom from resentment (courage)
8. confidence in the power of the teacher
9. confidence in one's own learning abilities
10. preparedness for deep learning

Program Structure and Implementation

The CII program consisted of nine (monthly) 50-minute presentations conducted at three different high schools throughout the school year. The program's main curriculum was guided by content from the primary textbook, *From the Browder File*. The book touches on a variety of subjects such as the history and psychological dynamics related to culture, politics, science, and health as viewed from an African-centered perspective. Some of the essays discussed included: "The Creation of Negro," "The Mother of Mankind," "On the Color Black," "Becoming a Born Again African," "Youth's Responsibility to the Future," "A Conversation With Dr. King," "The Politics of Hair," "Color, Culture, and Consciousness," among others.

The curriculum was designed to strengthen each student's knowledge and understanding of their African and African American heritage, which was particularly important because there were seldom more than two or three Black students in the other classes they attended at school. It was delightful for the students participating in the CII to be in a classroom with all Black students and a Black teacher who exposed them to information that made many of them feel proud to be Black for the first time in their lives.

Jessica, an alumna of the program, provided the following feedback:

> *From the Browder File* has opened my eyes to bigger and greater things. I've learned more from the few chapters we read than I've learned in my history class. This has been an experience I won't forget and I hope others can experience this as well. Thank you for keeping me "woke" and teaching me things school wouldn't.

Students were particularly pleased to learn of a Black history that existed centuries before slavery and to learn that the Ancient Egyptians were Black Africans who made numerous contributions to culture and civilization thousands of years before their country was conquered by Europeans and Arabs. Cheryl, another student shared,

> Tony Browder enlightened me about the importance of knowing our history through the lens of leaders, triumphs, and foundations. It is imperative that our students, especially those of African ancestry, know their entire history and the contributions of Africans to humanity. CII provides our students, parents, and our staff with missing pieces of their story that are so essential in building a sense of efficacy, pride, and vision for the future.

In addition to the in-class meetings, there were several family/parent meetings where we discussed information being taught to the students and entertained questions from parents and other family members present. These intergenerational gatherings were hosted by ABEN, who provided dinner to ensure greater family participation.

ABEN also sponsored field trips for students, teachers, and chaperones. Two of these extracurricular activities included a trip to the Rosicrucian Egyptian Museum in San Jose where I led a tour of the exhibits and museum grounds and provided detailed information on the collection and the architecture of the museum. Students also participated in a weekend conference sponsored by Black Students of California United (BSCU), which featured students of African descent from the entire state. During spring break, a select number of students participated in an all-expense paid 3-day trip to Washington, DC. Several teachers and parents served as chaperones, and I conducted tours of the Smithsonian National Museum of African American History and Culture and the Smithsonian Museum of Natural History.

Students and chaperones were also treated to my *Egypt on the Potomac Field Trip of Washington, D.C.* where they witnessed evidence of African history and culture hidden in plain sight throughout the nation's capital. This trip was particularly enlightening because students had opportunities to see evidence of many of the things they had read about and discussed in class, and they had an opportunity to be in a city with a majority Black population. For many students, it was an unforgettable experience that gave them a glimpse of what the future held for them.

The CII also benefited from the research of Mr. Kweli Zukeri, a graduate student from Howard University who was hired by ABEN to conduct a quantitative study on the program's impact on its participants. Over the course of two years, Mr. Zukeri conducted pre- and post-interviews with several students and their parents to ascertain the efficacy of CII and its short-term and long-term benefits.

Mr. Zukeri's research became the subject of his master's thesis at Howard University Department of Psychology. Zukeri, Watkins, and Browder were astounded when they were informed by Zukeri's advisor, Dr. Wade Boykin, chair of Howard Psychology Department, that his thesis was the first graduate-level thesis on a high school program of this nature. Mr. Zukeri's research found that there was a statistically significant increase in factors related to participant heritage engagement and racial identity. He found that there was an increase in their level of awareness of their African ancestry marked by intellectual intelligence and capacity, agency, and knowledge production, and an increase in participant belief in the value and uniqueness of being Black or of African ancestry. There was also a positive and significant correlation found between participant expression level of these two factors and their cumulative GPA at the time of the end of the 2016–2017 school year (2021).

Mr. Zukeri's final evaluation report contained a thematic review and summary of three themes. Theme 1: Engagement with Africana heritage and awareness of curricular cultural hegemony—Learning about Africana heritage and history helped participants more meaningfully engage with their heritage and feel good about their racial/ethnic identity, and recognize that the American education system suppresses the full narrative and legacy of people of African descent. Theme 2: Program engagement—Meaningful connections and learning communities. Participants expressed strong engagement with and personal impact from CII due, in part, to a high level of participation in program-sponsored activities, which created learning spaces that allowed participants to engage more deeply with the program and program content through meaningful interactions. Theme 3: Knowing and growing—An awakening—Participants underwent a process of awakening, catalyzed by learning new or "hidden" information presented by the program. This was characterized by a burgeoning sense of empowerment, which was often expressed by efforts made to share the information.

Dr. Boykin was so pleased with Mr. Zukeri's research that he encouraged him to continue this research for his doctoral dissertation. On November 15,

2021, Zukeri successfully defended his dissertation on: *An Exploration of African Heritage Engagement and Racial Identity Development in Black High School Participants of an African-Centered Program* and won high praise from his dissertation committee. Zukeri's examination of the relationship between heritage engagement, racial identity, and academic achievement will continue as he evaluates the next iteration of CII as it expands from a California-based program to a national program.

The National Cultural Imperative Program

The success of CII in Northern California raised the question as to how many more high school students could benefit from a year-long program devoted strictly to teaching African and African American history. Browder and Watkins contemplated the existing program and expanded the in-school CII activities into a Saturday academy called the Cultural Imperative Program (CIP), which was conducted in a dozen schools and community centers across the United States.

In 2017, Mr. Browder's daughter, Atlantis, joined the team as the national director of the Cultural Imperative Program. Atlantis brought 20 years of experience as a middle school and high school teacher to the project along with her expertise as a curriculum development specialist as well as an Ella Baker trainer with the Children's Defense Fund's annual Freedom School National Training in Clinton, TN.

Armed with a love for both students and teaching, Atlantis turned a great local initiative into an excellent national program. She created a new curriculum for students and teachers, and developed monthly training programs for site coordinators, facilitators, and volunteers. As the CIP expanded, it dramatically transformed the lives of hundreds of students, their parents and siblings, and the residents of the communities in which they lived.

Every participant in CII and CIP began and ended each session reciting a pledge penned by Mr. Browder called "Transition 14," which declared:

In the beginning our ancestors knew not.
They studied.
For four thousand years they learned all there was to know.
They taught others.
Then came the Maafa—the Great Disaster.

Enslavers made it illegal for Africans to read and write.
They were forced to forget all they had learned and taught.
After 400 years of forgetting, they forgot they had forgotten.
That changes today.
I will remember for them.
I will read for them.
I will write for them.
I will teach for them.
I will make certain they are never forgotten again.

In conclusion, the cultural imperative speaks to the responsibility of every adult to know their history and culture, preserve it and pass it on to the next generation. ABEN's fueling of first the CII, then the CIP will have a significant impact on countless lives across this country and throughout the diaspora for many years to come.

Questions

Anthony Browder explains the CII as addressing the needs of self-determined people to define their actions, which, in turn, ensures the preservation of social behaviors, knowledge, beliefs, laws, customs, and traditions that will guarantee their capacity to grow and thrive for generations. Some examples of other kinds of cultural imperative programs are Knarratives and the AYA Institute.What are some cultural imperatives that you can connect to in your community? What are some online communities that serve this purpose? How can those organizations support your current projects?

References

Alexander, M. (2012). *The new Jim Crow: Mass incarceration in the age of colorblindness*. The New Press.

Browder, A. (1989). *From the Browder file: 22 essays on the African American experience*. Institute of Karmic Guidance.

Churchill, Ward. (1990). *The COINTELPRO papers: documents from the FBI's secret wars against domestic dissent*. Boston, MA: South End Press,

Clarke, J. H. (1992). *Africans at the crossroads: African world revolution*. Africa World Press. Trenton, NJ.

Welsing, F. C. (1991). *The Isis papers: The keys to the colors*. CW Publishing.

Hilliard, A. G. (1978). *Free your mind, return to the source: The african origin of civilization, a resource outline*. Urban Institute for Human Services.

Hilliard, A. G. (1997). *SBA: The reawakening of the African mind*. Makare Publishing.

Hilliard, A.G. (Ed.). (1990). *Infusion of African and African American content in the school curriculum*. Aaron Press.

Hilliard, A. (2002). *True of voice: The poetry of Listervelt Middleton*. Makore Publishing.

Lewis, S. (2020). *The legacy of John Henrik Clarke*. Makore Publishing.

[Free Our People]. (2014, December 29). *Free Your Mind (Return To The Source African Origins. Dr. Asa Hilliard* [Video]. YouTube. https://www.youtube.com/watch?v=RQGU2TSTo0A

Shomburg, A. (1926). "The Negro digs up his past." *African American Poetry (1870–1926): A digital anthology*. Retrieved April 8, 2023, from https://scalar.lehigh.edu/african-american-poetry-a-digital-anthology/arthur-a-schomburg-arturo-schomburg-the-negro-digs-up-his-past-1925

Winbush , R., & Wright, D. (Eds.). (2020). *The Osirus Papers: Reflections on the life and writings of Dr. Frances Cress Welsing*. Black Classic Press.

Zukeri, K. (2021). *An exploration of Africana heritage engagement and racial identity development in Black high school students that participate in African-centered programming* (Doctoral dissertation, Howard University).

FOUR

A Youth Perspective on ABEN: A Greene Scholar's Experience

Ayinde Olokotin, Alumni, Greene Scholars Program

Introduction

My relationship with A Black Education Network (ABEN) began on a summer afternoon when I was in 4th grade. I recall climbing into my mom's minivan on the way back from summer camp. To my surprise, in my seat, usually occupied by my little brother Iyanu, was a pair of slacks, a button-down shirt, and a paisley tie. Confused, I remember asking my mom what I needed my "fancy outfit" for, when, as far as I remembered, the next event was going to the pool or a friend's house, to which my mom responded, "Don't you remember? Today is your interview for the Greene Scholars Program!" That was the beginning of a journey that has molded my identity and trajectory as a becoming Black scholar.

The Greene Scholars Program, founded by ABEN's visionary Executive Director, Debra Watkins, was established to provide educational enrichment with a focus on science, technology, engineering, and mathematics (STEM) for students of African ancestry in the Bay Area. Although I doubt the 4th-grade version of me would have been able to give you the aforementioned definition of the Greene Scholars Program, I definitely would have been able to tell you the mantra emphatically repeated by the program's teachers and directors. Since I was in elementary school, the mission of the Greene Scholars Program has been to ensure that Black students are "not only STEM competent, but STEM confident." Since I was in elementary school, the ethos of the Greene Scholars Program has remained constant: The goal is never to be proficient. The goal is to be excellent.

Throughout my academic journey, the Greene Scholars Program has grounded me in a community of peers and jegna who have exemplified, encouraged, and inspired academic excellence and social responsibility. Furthermore, the Bay Area is a politically charged educational environment marred by stereotype threat, so for me and many of my peers, the Greene Scholars Program was an intellectual respite where we were constantly reminded that we did not succeed *in spite* of our Blackness, but through the resilience, love, and model of Black excellence imparted by the leadership of the Greene Scholars Program.

The role of the Greene Scholars Program for Black youth in America cannot be underscored enough. Subject to the racism that manifests within the classroom from the outset of their education, to be a Black child in the American educational system is to have a congenital disadvantage. A group of researchers, led by Yale professor Walter Gilliam, showed 135 educators videos of children in a classroom setting. Each video had a Black boy and girl, and a White boy and girl. The teachers were subsequently given a directive to detect "challenging behavior" exhibited by the students, despite the non-existence of such "challenging behavior" in any of the videos. Nevertheless, when asked which children required the most attention, 42% of the teachers identified the Black boy. The participants' conscious appraisal of whom they believed required the most attention coincided with the independent results of an eye-tracking technology used by the research team, which recorded that preschool teachers "show a tendency to more closely observe Black students, especially boys, when challenging behaviors are expected" (Samuels, 2016).

The Yale Child Study Center's experiment indexing implicit bias in preschools provides an overwhelming amount of anecdotal and analytical evidence that the American education system is as instrumental as its criminal justice, healthcare, and other counterparts in the American sociopolitical landscape in the perpetuation of racism and White supremacy, particularly at the expense of Black youth.

However, when our educational system pedagogically and socially fails Black children, it is programs like the Greene Scholars that take it upon themselves to ensure that failure does not beget more failure, empowering Black students to transcend the myriad barriers of the classroom. On the website, the mission statement of ABEN states its goal is to "assist our children and youth in reaching their full potential by facilitating academic and cultural excellence wherever they are." In this respect, the Greene Scholars Program is a paragon of ABEN's mission. Along every step of the path in my academic journey, the Greene Scholars Program was there to bolster my confidence, expand my opportunities, and ground my academic and career aspirations in a strong sense of personal and collective identity.

My earliest memories of the Greene Scholars Program consist of engrossing physics experiments, competing with my peers to see who could build the fastest marble ramps with Ms. Christina, and listening intently as Gloria Whitaker-Daniels (program director of the Greene Scholars Program at the time) told us about the latest Amazon technology she was developing.

However, predictably (for anyone who knows me personally), my favorite early memory of the Greene Scholars Program was my first science fair. The Greene Scholars Program's annual science fair is the showcase event of the year. Following weeks of research, experimentation, and analysis, the science fair is the day where Greene Scholars have the opportunity to display the findings of their hypothesis or innovation-driven project to their peers, families, judges, and the public. After spending weeks developing and testing my project, examining pigmentation solvency differences through chromatography, I remember bursting with excitement walking into the science fair with my board that I had stayed up all night perfecting (until 2 AM if I remember correctly . . . as an 8-year-old whose bedtime was at 8 PM, that was a memorable detail). I remember seeing Black kids everywhere, proudly displaying their scientific experiments, just like me. I was used to being the only Black kid in the classroom. Still, more importantly, I was used to people being surprised that I was smart, that I had intellectual depth, so walking into a room where that was the *norm* for kids that looked like me was ineffable; it felt like something out of a movie. I will never forget that feeling, and I remember presenting my project on chromatography, a complex scientific phenomenon for a 4th grader to explain, not only with competence, but with *confidence*.

The following day was the Greene Scholars science fair gala, where the program's students, volunteers, and patrons were celebrated, and most importantly (to my 4th-grade self), where the science fair winners were announced. I remember sitting on the edge of my seat for what felt like centuries until they called out the science fair awards. The emcee announced, "Third place" . . . not me. "Second place" . . . not me. "First place" . . . not me. I felt devastated. He continued, ". . . and the grand prize goes to . . . Ayinde Olukotun." I hadn't known there would be a grand prize!

I will always remember the moment my 8-year-old self stumbled up to the stage to accept the green trophy. Since that day, I have won five more Greene Scholars science fair grand prizes and I have presented various findings at the Synopsys Santa Clara County Science Fair, and the California State Science Fair, with invitations to present at the Raytheon National Science Fair, because I have strived to make the little boy standing up on the stage, beaming, holding his little green trophy, proud. That boy is a product of the Greene Scholars Program.

Though salient in my experience in the Greene Scholars Program, the science fair was just one of the many ways the program encouraged academic excellence and a depth of understanding of STEM concepts, with monthly programs dedicated to disciplines from neuroscience and geometry to chemistry and biomedical engineering. In the biomedical engineering unit, one of the most memorable opportunities I had was the chance to learn about, and subsequently build, prosthetic limbs. To me, learning about and modeling this medical innovation that has transformed so many people's lives so profoundly epitomizes the approach of the Greene Scholars Program: A hands-on learning experience about science, technology, engineering, and mathematics, grounded in an understanding of the capacity it has, and that you have by extension, to better the lives of people around you. That is one of the principle reasons why the Greene Scholars Program is so unique. In contextualizing the study of STEM with its potential for making the community better, the Greene Scholars Program produces scholars that are not only academically grounded, but also morally, with a critical understanding of the role of science and technology in increasing social responsibility.

Unfortunately, to fully comprehend the necessity of the Greene Scholars Program, understanding the significance of these lessons being taught in a space where Black students, like myself, could learn and engage intellectually without being impeded by stereotype threat is crucial. As defined by J.L. Smith, stereotype threat "is a situational experience in which an individual feels vulnerable and pressured by the possibility of confirming or being judged by a stereotype. The threatening experience leads to performance decrements, even among highly skilled individuals" (2004, p. 177). In their experiment analyzing the generalizability of stereotype threat effects, Claude Steele, Steven Spencer, and Joshua Aaronson (2002) examined how group stereotypes threaten how students evaluate themselves. This leads to altered academic identity and intellectual performance. This social-psychological phenomenon has the potential to negatively impact members of any group about whom negative stereotypes exist. To quantify this theory, Steele gave Black and White college students a half-hour test using difficult items from the verbal Graduate Record Exam (GRE). In the stereotype-threat condition, student subjects were told that the test "diagnosed intellectual ability, thus potentially eliciting the stereotype that Black students are less intelligent than White students" (p. 382). In the condition devoid of stereotype threat, the researchers told students that the test was a "problem-solving lab task that said nothing about ability, presumably rendering stereotypes irrelevant" (p. 382). Under the stereotype-threat condition, Black students, matched with their White peers using SAT scores, performed markedly worse than their White counterparts. However, when there was no stereotype-threat condition—the exact same test was described as a lab task that, ostensibly was decoupled from racist stereotypes about Black people's intelligence—the Black students' performance matched that of their White counterparts (Steele et al., 2002).

The tragic reality is that you cannot "self-confidence" your way out of systemic racism, and to expect Black children, still in their formative years, to do so is ultimately setting them up for failure. Therein lies the necessity of the Greene Scholars Program's status as an affinity space for students of African ancestry in the Bay Area.

I want to clarify that none of this is to say that families should concede defeat and accept that the internalization of these White supremacist lies is impervious to any efforts to deconstruct them. Quite the opposite. I hope any parents of Black children reading this are reminded of how critical it is to take every opportunity to explicitly affirm their children's identity, intellect, and self-image within their Blackness. I hope this imparts a sense of urgency: To prevent Black children from internalizing notions of racial inferiority regarding their intellect, we have no other option but to actively fight such normative societal messaging. Nevertheless, the reality of stereotype threat is such that in environments where Black students can learn with peers that look like them, they can engage intellectually as individuals rather than as involuntary proxies for their race. Learning in Black spaces allows Black students to pursue learning independent of centuries of White supremacist falsehoods about Black intellect. Although many Black children won't be able articulate it, I know I certainly couldn't at that young age, they too know the feeling I felt walking into the science fair, and how palpably different it felt than walking into a classroom where the pressure of being a "prototypical" Black student is omnipresent. It's the difference between feeling like a specimen and feeling like a student.

The functions of the Greene Scholars Program, as part of its mission to ensure holistic success for its students, is by no means circumscribed within

STEM fields. In addition to the provision of a safe space for intellectual engagement for Black scholars, the Greene Scholars Program offers numerous opportunities for scholars to foster relationships with established Black professionals through events like the annual career fair and workshops such as resume building. These ensure that Greene Scholars are well equipped to navigate the corporate world adeptly. Additionally, prior to matriculation to higher education, the Greene Scholars Program generously gifts thousands of dollars in scholarships and prizes to graduating scholars to ensure that college tuition fees are less financially prohibitive for students and families; they reward commitment to academic excellence, service of one's community, and engagement with the Greene Scholars Program and its history through essay competitions.

However, equally as crucial as the Greene Scholars Program's dedication to academic excellence is its unwavering commitment to the sociopolitical advancement of the Black community, or "*cultural* excellence" as ABEN would term it, amongst its scholars. Central to the Greene Scholars Program were initiatives and lessons that ensured that we were never culturally deracinated; through activities like the Black History Bowl, competitions based on knowledge of Black history, the Greene Scholars program ensured that all Greene scholars had a depth of understanding and respect for the ancestors and pioneers who made the conditions for our current aspirations possible. The notion that we stand upon the shoulders of our ancestors and have the responsibility to build upon their dreams for the sake of future generations has always been a cornerstone of the ethos of the Greene Scholars Program.

Through the impactful work of my fellow Greene Scholars alumni, even today we have seen those dreams begin to be realized by the youth. I've spent time discussing the profound impact the leadership and teachers of the Greene Scholars Program had on me, but equally as significant in my experience were the brilliant peers I was surrounded by, not only from an academic perspective, but, more importantly in my eyes, from an ethical and social justice perspective. The Greene Scholars Program's focus on community service, social responsibility, and strength of collective identity meant that my fellow Greene Scholars were as committed to the welfare of our community as they were to the academic excellence they pursued.

To name a salient example, Nyla Choates, a fellow Greene Scholars Program alumna, founded the nonprofit My Roots Are Rich. Her nonprofit's mission is to "empower, inspire, and educate people by reinforcing the rich culture of African Americans and their contributions to America." Her first book, named *My Roots are Rich*, tells the story of how a young girl who has low self image blossoms once she is introduced to the richness of her culture. Choates contends that reading for enjoyment, historical context and factual knowledge builds social, literacy, and language skills. Due to the COVID-19 outbreak, she shares, many young children of color did not have the opportunity to improve or expand their reading and reading comprehension skills due to various social disparities. The mission of My Roots are Rich is to help close this literacy gap, one book at a time with pre-recorded videos of Choates reading short stories.

Furthermore, in addition to various nonprofits and organizations founded by Greene Scholars to redress social injustice and myriad manifestations of systemic racism, numerous Greene Scholars engage in community organization, many of them mobilizing their communities in the wake of the successive murders of Breonna Taylor, George Floyd, Ahmaud Arbery, with several scholars organizing protests totaling tens of thousands of people all over the Bay Area. I was one of them. When Ahmaud Arbery was murdered, I remember thinking that I would need time to mentally and emotionally process his murder before I could respond or mobilize in any meaningful way. Then Breonna Taylor was murdered in her own home. Again, I knew I would need time to mentally and emotionally process her murder before I could respond or mobilize in any meaningful way. And then George Floyd was murdered, and I realized that America would allow me no time to mentally or emotionally recuperate before doing something. The Greene Scholars Program was part of my social justice foundation that empowered me to organize a Black Lives Matter protest in June of 2020 attended by elected and community leaders, including U.S. Rep. Anna Eshoo, Palo Alto Mayor Adrian Fine, East Palo Alto Mayor Regina Wallace-Jones, author and activist Julie Lythcott-Haims, and trailblazing judge LaDoris Cordell; it was documented to be the largest organized protest in Palo Alto history.

Furthermore, the principles instilled in me by the Greene Scholars Program regarding commitment to community welfare empowered me to stand up to the police department in Palo Alto, speaking out against their racist policing tactics, asserting to the Palo Alto police chief that "It's easy to discuss systemic racism in abstraction and talk about its nationwide implications, but we have to remember that the goals of movements like Black Lives Matter are rooted in tangible action, action in communities, namely to address police brutality. And because of that, I feel that it would be morally and intellectually irresponsible not to discuss the manifestation of police brutality, racism, and bigotry in my own community."

My confrontation with the Palo Alto police chief was ultimately the product of years of racial profiling, suspect brutalization, and broader departmental misconduct that has been, essentially, an open secret in my hometown of Palo Alto. However, it was catalyzed by the brutalization of a man named Julio Arevalo by Agent Thomas DeStefano, who has been named in three lawsuits for using excessive force, including a case leading to the largest settlement in recent Palo Alto city history. Surveillance footage from that case shows the Palo Alto police department once again engaging in police brutality. The footage shows the plaintiff leaving a store with a doughnut before Agent DeStefano approached him in the parking lot. As the plaintiff walked back toward the entrance of the store, "DeStefano shoved him against a metal railing several times and threw him face-down onto the ground." The suit claims that the plaintiff briefly lost consciousness, while in the surveillance footage, "his feet flailed while DeStefano knelt on top of him." The suit states that DeStefano claimed in a police report that he had seen the plaintiff "complete a hand-to-hand drug transaction with a man in the parking lot." This was uncorroborated by the surveillance footage, which showed the plaintiff "talking to a woman and two men outside the shop before DeStefano approached him, but they did not touch." A subsequent internal Palo Alto police investigation determined that DeStefano had acted reasonably, according to the suit, and rejected the plaintiff's initial November 2019 claim of excessive force. The officer responsible for overseeing the investigation was a groomsman in Agent DeStefano's wedding (Kelliher, 2020).

Armed with the values instilled in me by the years of leadership and support in the Greene Scholars Program, I remember telling the Palo Alto police chief, in a public forum meeting, that "Agent DeStefano has not been fired. The legislative inaction and refusal to punish police misconduct being exhibited by the governing powers of Palo Alto can be described as nothing other than malfeasance. I would be ashamed as a public official with a fiduciary responsibility to my community, to leave a legacy so marred by moral bankruptcy, because as long as officers with track records of bigotry and brutality are protected and promoted within the Palo Alto police department, you have failed me, and every single one of your constituents along with me." The courage I found to take a stand in defense of my community was built upon a foundation of moral convictions that the Greene Scholars program helped lay.

Conclusion

Where it concerns the indelible mark the Greene Scholars program has left on my personal, academic, and career aspirations, I would be remiss not to discuss Debra Watkins, the founder of the Greene Scholars Program. A luminary of Black education, a jegna, and a personal model because of the dedication of her life's work to the welfare of her community, when I think of champions of Black education, the name Debra Watkins will always be transcendent.

My relationship with Ms. Watkins is perhaps what I cherish most when reflecting upon the numerous blessings that have stemmed from my time in the Greene Scholars Program. Ever since I was young, I remember her being my fiercest ally, always there to commend me on my achievements and to challenge me to aspire to the highest level of intellectual excellence. Coming from a lineage of service, which I was able to explore by writing about the legacy of her mother, Rosie Mae Masters, Ms. Watkins was pivotal in the development of the scholar and the person I am today. From her constant encouragement and support during my time in the Greene Scholars Program, her generosity with scholarships for my tuition at Pomona College, and continuous advocacy for me to further pursue my intellectual goals, I could not have envisioned an advocate, in every sense of the meaning, as phenomenal as Ms. Watkins.

Most recently, having selected me to be in her inaugural class of Youth Civic Ambassadors for Justice, I would like to think my research is a testament to the vision of the Greene Scholars Program insofar as it is to pursue intellectual goals that allow a person to uphold the welfare of the community, in my case, combating systemic efforts to disenfranchise Black people. In addition to conducting policy research for the Office of Anna Eshoo regarding voter suppression, I'm currently authoring an analytical paper examining how, subsequent to the 2008 election of Barack Obama, the Republican Party realized they did not have a demographic future in this country. Thus, I am examining how Republicans engaged in a concerted effort at the national and state levels to disenfranchise Black people in this country.

Speaking from the perspective of an alumnus of the Greene Scholars Program who has matriculated through the program over the course of more than a decade, I can attest to the enduring role the Greene Scholars Program has had on my personal, professional, and academic trajectory. From the very beginning of my education through my high school graduation and beyond, the Greene Scholars Program was there to model Black excellence, in all of its beautiful modes and manifestations. Still, most importantly, the Greene Scholars Program was there to help me achieve it for myself, and that is something for which I will forever be indebted.

Questions

Have you talked to participants in your organization and members of your community about your organization, school, and/or program? What is the value added for them? What are they saying about the imprint your work has left on them?

References

Kelliher, F. (2020, June 26,). Palo Alto police face Federal lawsuit alleging excessive force, pattern of abuse. *The Mercury News*. https://www.mercurynews.com/2020/06/25/palo-alto-police-face-federal-lawsuit-alleging-excessive-force-pattern-of-abuse/

Samuels, C. (2016). Early childhood: "Do early educators' implicit biases regarding sex and race relate to behavior expectations and recommendations of preschool expulsions and suspensions?" *Education Week, 36*(8), 5.

Smith, J. L. (2004). Understanding the process of stereotype threat: A review of mediational variables and new performance goal directions. *Educational Psychology Review, 16*(3), 177–206. https://doi.org/10.1023/B:EDPR.0000034020.20317.89

Steele, C. M., Spencer, S. J., & Aronson, J. (2002). Contending with group image: The psychology of stereotype and social identity threat. *Advances in Experimental Social Psychology, 34*, 379–440.

FIVE

Two Minds and One Vision: Reflections from Mama Rosaline Preudhomme, the Keeper of Wisdom

Rona M. Frederick, PhD

GLORIA ROSALINE PREUDHOMME, LOVINGLY REFERRED to as Mama Roz, spent her time in service to those most disenfranchised in New York City. One of her more recent endeavors was simple yet profound: to end the war on drugs through the reform of marijuana legislation. Mama Roz has served as a lifelong advocate for children, working alongside 50 youth-serving agencies to implement program activities for the New York City site of the National Funding Collaborative on Violence Prevention. Beginning in 1995 and until her recent retirement, she had been implementing rites of passage programming in Detroit, New York, Philadelphia, Toronto, and Miami. Rites of passage programs support youth in transitioning to manhood or womanhood.

Mama Roz is originally from Barbados. However, she has spent much of her life in Brooklyn, NY. Debra Watkins and Mama Roz share the same North Star—betterment for and self-determination of the African community in the United States and abroad. Those who know and love Mama Roz and her activism recognize her as a pioneer, an educator, and an advocate for Black children. Like her parents, she was an accomplished teacher, and her passion for teaching is ever present. Like Debra Watkins, while teaching, Mama Roz was constantly encouraged by those who beseeched her to leave the classroom so she could replicate her outstanding work for the masses of children in New York City schools. Her legacy in New York includes designing the career intern program, working in administration at the Board of Education, and serving as the deputy commissioner in the New York State Office of Children for more than 12 years. In 2013, she was recognized by the New York State Senate with a Pan-African Legacy Award for her lifetime commitment to marginalized communities.

Now in her mid-70s, Mama Roz has a peaceful, grounded presence. As she speaks, each cadence is marked with intention and it is clear to the listener why she is known by some as "the keeper of wisdom." She thoughtfully shares that she embraces lessons learned from her experience and is ready to serve as a steady thought partner for those committed to changing the trajectory of Black children's lives. In the book, *We Live for the We: The Political Power of Black Motherhood*, Dani McClain, writer at *The Nation*, describes Mama Roz as an "activist who has been on the front lines in battles ranging from the Brooklyn chapter of the Congress of Racial Equality (CORE) to efforts to desegregate the Ocean Hill-Brownsville schools." McClain (2019) captures Mama Roz's spirit when she elaborates on the wise words shared during their exchange. Mama Roz said growing up in a small village in Barbados taught her the power of the extended community and fictive kinship, which disrupts the narrow inward focus on the nuclear family and expands the notion of caregiver to all capable and willing adults. Mama Roz offered this sage advice to McClain: "You must find your village." By this she means "a community that loves, supports, and respects you. They will hold you up." These words best capture her role as an elder in the community. Mama Roz, who began her early education in a one-room schoolhouse surrounded by loving elders who cared deeply for the children, pays this experience forward. With a focus on Black excellence and high standards, she continues to hold the community up.

Mama Roz's belief in the village concept naturally connected her to Debra Watkins. Initially, she had heard of Watkins while desperately trying to serve the fostered and orphaned Haitian children who were educationally languishing after the devastation of the 2010 hurricane. Through her work with the Institute of Black World 21st Century, she helped mobilize Black organizations to support recovery efforts. During a call with leaders from Black organizations across the nation who were organizing specific support for the children of Haiti, one leader shared that "there is a dynamo in Northern California who would be interested in the cause." That dynamo was Debra Watkins. Mama Roz recalls that Watkins began to attend the meetings and poured her wisdom and resources into the effort to save the children of Haiti. Mama Roz was amazed as she observed Debra Watkins' leadership. It wasn't until years later that they would connect on a more personal level.

Relationship-building is one of the key components of networking, and yet, sometimes the most important connections occur unexpectedly. A person may leave a small imprint that, over time, becomes an indelible mark. This held true for Debra Watkins and Mama Roz. When Mama Roz's grandson readied himself to attend college at Stanford University, the family did not know anyone in California. Mama Roz was reminded of Debra Watkins and reached out. Watkins' reception was warm, and she took in Mama Roz's grandson as if he were her own. It was clear that the like-minded visionaries and activists both shared a belief in the metaphoric village and fictive kinship. For those Africans who are committed, community uplift transcends geographic location, time, and the need for familiarity. Mama Roz commented that as Debra Watkins adopted her grandson, Mama Roz and her daughter adopted Debra Watkins. Eventually, their relationship circled back to their professional work in Black communities.

When Mama Roz and Debra Watkins met, they discussed the nature of the educational spaces in New York. They discussed key community stakeholders and they focused on the needs of Black school children. Debra Watkins recognized Mama Roz's abundant knowledge and connections to the community and solicited her help. Simultaneously, Mama Roz acknowledged the good work of ABEN and was excited to bring its signature programming to New York City. As their discussions continued, Debra Watkins wanted Mama Roz to have a permanent role with ABEN focused on education, programs, and policy. Mama Roz explained that much of her work was identifying "spaces and places and individuals that I know have already demonstrated their commitment to Black excellence."

Their union would bridge ABEN's work from the East to the West coast. As Debra Watkins made inroads in New York, Mama Roz, along with her networks, was poised to support her in expanding ABEN's work in New York schools. The relationship was mutually beneficial, balanced, and purposeful as both women had laser-sharp focus on Black excellence and high standards. Mama Roz shared,

> There is no substitute for excellence. Set a standard at being the best at all that you do . . . Black excellence is seeking to bring out the best. Debra lives, breathes, promotes, sleeps, and dreams in [high standards] in everything she does. (R. Preudhomme, personal communication, May 26, 2021)

One of their first initiatives included building out ABEN's presence in New York city schools. Mama Roz was impressed by Anthony Browder's cultural imperative program. She immediately invited Browder, his daughter Atlantis, and Debra Watkins to deliver a presentation to a group of educators in New York. As a result, two schools have adopted and are running the program.

Mama Roz also knew that the virtual Ghana tours would provide much needed exposure to life in other parts of the world for the children of New York City, who had been quarantined for months. In 2020, New York was at the epicenter of the COVID-19 Pandemic which, during its peak, claimed the lives of hundreds daily. Through Mama Roz's relationships with school districts in New York City, she was able to select a school in Far Rockaway where the children had not only been deeply affected by COVID-19, but also by Hurricane Sandy in years prior. Eighty percent of the students lived in temporary housing where Wi-Fi was spotty and technology was scarce. However, with the support of the principal and scholarships from ABEN, the virtual trip was implemented successfully. Mama Roz shared that the virtual tour was an outstanding experience, and the principal added that her students were forever transformed by it. The bestselling Amazon book, *WE DID THAT!: Traveling to Ghana During the 2020 Pandemic*, documents their journey.

Mama Roz, inspired by the ABEN Summer Institutes, wanted to provide opportunities for the Black principals of New York to experience the professional development. In the summer of 2021, Mama Roz and Debra Watkins offered a scholarship to one New York City principal to attend the Institute. Two others, excited about the Institutes, paid their own way. Mama Roz recalls that the principals were blown away by presentations by Drs. Bettina Love, Joyce King, Iva Carruthers, and others. One principal wrote as her final message on the Zoom chat, "I will return! Thank you!" Mama Roz noticed that during and immediately following the Institute, social media feeds were abuzz as the attending principal raved about the Institute to her network of Black principals in New York City. Immediately Mama Roz and the Black principals began to discuss how they could replicate the ABEN Summer Institute as a professional development opportunity in New York City for principals and teachers.

The future holds great possibilities for New York schools and ABEN. Mama Roz looks back at the lessons learned and opportunities gained with deep satisfaction. She embodies gratitude as she speaks of the work she does with and for ABEN. Now, in the autumn of her career, she still welcomes the opportunity to learn, grow, and serve the community she loves most. She shares that she is a committed and ready partner to Debra Watkins and is excited about the strategic partnership. Moreover, she is thankful for the continued work she is doing to enhance the lives of Black children in New York.

Question

Some would argue that networking is awkward and therefore, they avoid it at all cost. In the case of Debra Watkins and Rosalind Preudhomme, it was a natural synergy that led to an invaluable strategic partnership. How do you network with like-minded individuals? What are your steps to forging meaningful strategic relationships that serve your target audience?

References

McClain, D. (2019). *We live for the we: The political power of Black motherhood.* Bold Type Books.

Watkins, D. & Utsey, M. (Eds.) *WE DID THAT!: Traveling to Ghana during the 2020 pandemic.* ABEN.

SIX

The Power of the ABEN Summer Institutes: The Village Method

Rona M. Frederick, PhD

ABEN inspired a greater hope, faith and belief that we can create something specific for our area. ABEN provided powerful messaging and invested allies in the Black community. This network increased the impact and implementation of our work.

—*The Gaskins (M. Gaskins, personal communication, May 20, 2021)*

The Gaskins: Founders of the Village Method

The Gaskins' love story for the Black community is simple and their intentions are pure. They could easily finish each other's sentences, but choose instead to listen respectfully, building on the power of each other's thoughts and experiences. Mahea offers a thoughtful, spiritual presence: Her cadence brims with sincerity, depth, and clarity, and leaves listeners wanting more. Mark is a powerful presence, moving forward with intention and purpose. His work and passion stem from years of deep study, care for African people, and a love of God. Mark, like Mahea, is grounded in the knowledge that African people derive from a legacy of rich thought and educational excellence. Both accept the calling to facilitate intergenerational cultural transmission, recognizing that they are an integral part of a proud tradition of African people deeply dedicated to building with and for the community. They created The Village Method (TMV), an afterschool program in Northern California, with a sense of purpose and patience, care, and respect for Black children.

Mahea and Mark Gaskins founded TVM in 2014 as a nonprofit designed to work with schools to provide direct services to Black students attending schools in Southern Alameda County. Located in the San Francisco Bay area, Alameda derived its name from a Spanish word meaning "tree lined" with a stream that ran throughout. Alameda County includes cities like Union City, Oakland, Berkeley, and Albany with a mix of urban and suburban spaces.

Union City boasts a population of over 75,000. Demographically, the city's largest ethnic groups are Asian (54%); White (20% non-Hispanic); Hispanic

(22%); and Black (5%) (Union City, n.d.). The small percentage of Blacks in Union City reflects the reality of many small towns, cities, and enclaves in California where Blacks are a scattered minority.

Thus, a "village" to support the small number of Black students in this school district was important to both Mahea and Mark not only for the Black youth in Alameda, but for them as parents and as community organizers. The proverb, "it takes a village" (trite and misused in many circles) represented the perfect metaphor for this couple. Grounded in an African worldview, Fu-Kiau and Lukondo Wamba (Kindezi) demonstrate that the proverb 'it takes a village' is really about raising a village, not a child. In this case, being a part of a village is a sacred calling. All members—parents, caregivers, educators, and other supporters—are valued. Accordingly, children feel a sense of belonging and protection; only then can the village thrive.

As such, TVM organization forms protective barriers around their Black youth and coaches cohorts of students through the school pipeline, ensuring academic achievement and access to programming in their public school. The organization began with about 45 youth, which was approximately 33% of the 6th-grade Black students in their town. By the second year, they worked with 60 youth. By 2016, TVM served over one-third of Union City middle school students of African ancestry, with volunteers dedicating nearly 1,000 hours of support to their students. Currently, TVM has impacted 300 students and is supporting the transition of its first class to college. In a nutshell, the Gaskins explain that:

> . . . we push into schools, and then we celebrate culture and we use the curriculum that Mahea would create. We would invite other thought leaders, teachers and professionals, whether they be dancers or staffers or artists, musicians, poets, authors. We bring in people and share them not just with the youth, but with their families as well. We try to inspire the celebration and the positive contributions that come from our culture and to turn it into something that is more of a necessity. (M. Gaskins, personal communication, May 20, 2021)

TVM's mission is to make youth unstoppable by offering culturally responsive youth development, family engagement, and community outreach programming in South Alameda County and is exemplified by their intentional logo. The Adinkra symbol *eban* literally translates to "fence," which is a symbol of security, love, and protection. A fence affords protection and is thereby associated with the safety one finds in love. The color green represents life, hope, and vitality. TVM offers love, protection, and life. The Kwanzaa principle *umoja* represents unity, attaching to one another and to values as a community. The yellow represents the wealth, glory, and preciousness of African people. The story of African culture and history includes those of people who suffered, struggled, and fought for every achievement gained. The spears of the logo represent the village's willingness to struggle and fight for their children and community, as well as the strength derived from the past. Both Mahea and Mark emphatically share that they "recognize the brilliance of Black children!"

It is evident that the Gaskins' work is deeply spiritual and mission driven. Much like the jegnas in the traditional African Dagara community in Burkino Fasa, the Gaskins agree their purpose is twofold: to recognize and awaken the brilliance of Black children and to facilitate the delivery of genius into the community (Some, 1998). Mark, with intention, states:

> We find ways to harness the energy and show that [Black children and their] ways are powerful] because of the way [they] are naturally made. We simultaneously heal and tap into the special gifts and talents of the children we serve. (M. Gaskins, personal communication, May 20, 2021)

With support from ABEN and similarly oriented organizations, the Gaskins' vision to build systems to liberate Black children was realized.

Their ideas were inspired by luminaries like James Comer, a child psychiatrist at Yale who founded the highly successful Comer School Development Program, Asa Hilliard, and Wade Nobles. Mahea took classes with both Baba Asa Hilliard III, who was her professor and later, department chair and dean of Education at San Francisco State University; and Wade Nobles, who founded the Institute for the Advanced Study of Black Family, Life, and Culture. Together, Mahea and Mark drew from their life experiences, lessons learned from the heroic efforts of Geoffrey Canada, and readings from elders like Jawanza Kunjufu and Wade Boykins, all leaders in African-centered thought and practice, to create the mission of TVM.

Several consequential experiences occurred to drive these grassroots organizers to create TVM. In 2008, upon graduating from Berkeley, Mahea worked for R.T. Fisher Educational Enterprises, which sent droves of teachers and staff to CAAAE/ABEN's Summer Institute at Stanford University to deepen their thinking around cultural awareness, thought, and practice. Mahea shares, "I recall going to ABEN's Summer Institute years ago with a coworker when I worked for an educational consulting firm and we both were blown away!" Her coworker often reminds Mahea that at the Institute, Mahea said she was going to create a way to bring like-minded Africans together to build a community (which would later become TVM). Mahea does not recall saying that, but in retrospect, she believes her coworker. The seeds of TVM were planted.

Meanwhile, Mark was working in the technology industry where he noticed disturbing patterns for Black children in Alameda County that troubled his spirit. He noticed a lot of gang violence, which came to head on December 21, 2007, when Vernon Eddins, Jr. was murdered outside of his school by gang members. The community was shaken. Based on conversations with the children they tutored at church, both Mark and Mahea realized that the young people did not know what village they were from nor did they have a support network. The response from the community was to treat the students as if they were responsible for the death of their friend. Vernon's mom sued the school system, and eventually the school district was deemed responsible for not keeping Black children safe. For Mark, this was a turning point. As a father with a young family, the ideas started to churn.

As their son got older and entered the public school system, they plaintively stated, "our own son's light was dimming. I guess you never know how you are going to face the boogeyman until you are standing in front of the boogeyman? And so the stereotypes and racism and how some cultures, some people look at Black boys, Black men, it really hit me head on." Later Mark added, "this is one of our greatest investments, our son. And we're putting him in a system that I honestly don't have faith in. I didn't know how to actually protect him and how to help him" (M. Gaskins, personal communication, May 20, 2021).

In 2011, the Gaskins embarked on a listening tour to identify the issues plaguing Black youth in Alameda County. Their driving question was: How is the community supporting Black children? They spoke with the school district, health agencies, political leaders, the police department, directors of recreational centers, and city leaders, collecting as much data as possible. And they listened. They realized that there was limited programming and very little support for Black students in a county that was rich with resources for others. They experienced a lot of pushback from schools who were unwilling to "let them in." They also noticed a lot of assimilation among the few Black teachers who worked in Alameda County and Black teachers that experienced a high burnout rate. Moreover, the hostility was palpable. They realized they were alone. They recognized the need for buy-in and support systems. Like many conscious grassroots organizers located in predominantly White spaces, they felt as though they were by themselves, with an extremely arduous task of liberating Black children within a racially hostile place. No one would help. Other parts of CA were networking. But not in their county.

Despite exhaustion, racialized trauma, and the challenges of being a young couple raising their own small children, they dreamed of the possibilities for the Black community. Giving up was not an option; their children—all children were at stake. They were "lit up" by the larger mission and legacy of which they were a part, and by the tragic circumstances of Black children. Mark expressed that coming out of enslavement:

> Beyond Tulsa, we built thriving Black townships all over the country with love, peace, joy and integrity—the soul of the African . . . [our ancestors] figured out a formula [that supported within] community a preference for one another—the calling together—movement with action. (M. Gaskins, personal communication, May 20, 2021)

Mark recognized the possibilities and acknowledged the legacy. What he needed was support. Seeking answers, the Gaskins joined the African American Student Achievement Initiative (AASAI) founded by the school district and led by Diane Levy, who was fondly referred to as "Mama Diana". Mama Diana was a strong supporter and ally of ABEN. As a result of joining the initiative organization, Mark was introduced to CAAAE/ABEN and began attending its Institutes. He shared that they eventually got passes (from Mama Diana) to go as parents to the ABEN Institutes at Stanford. Whereas Mahea was introduced to ABEN as a teacher/practitioner years prior, Mark attended as a parent and concerned community leader. Collectively, Mark and Mahea found the support they needed through ABEN and other like-minded organizations.

ABEN became their watering hole, a place of nourishment and meaningful connections. Coming out of their silo in Alameda County, which Mark refers to as a "cultural desert" (especially for African-centered thinkers), to attend the ABEN Institutes was an answered prayer. As creative individuals and institution builders, they found both inspiration and much of what they needed at ABEN. They recalled a network of resources and a place from which to draw energy. They also found people who were further down the road they were currently on. There were also vendors present at the Institutes. They continued to add that they connected with Ashay by the Bay, a Black bookseller because they had the most beautiful resources and books, and other material that they drew from and immediately applied to their work.

The Gaskins built relationships with like-minded warriors at ABEN that further informed their practices. Through ABEN, their network and practice grew. Gaskins added that the ABEN Institutes offered not only immediate support but also long-term relationships. These relationships sustained their work and shifted their psychic spaces as parents, warriors, and healers as they engaged daily in racial combat in Southern Alameda County. Two of the most valued relationships fostered by ABEN were with Baba Wekesa Madzimoyo and Mama Afiya Madzimoyo of AYA, who taught them to explore their feelings of systemic racism through the AYA Educational Institute's powerful Warriors, Healers, and Builders training brought to the West Coast by ABEN. Warriors, Healers, Builders is a multigenerational journey designed to counter the psychological damage of institutionalized racism and to provide a path that enables participants to explore the messages feelings send, to gain tools to address hurts and pains, and to bring participants toward greater feelings of joy, peace and power. The ultimate goal is African sovereignty. This connection proved to be life-changing for the Gaskins. Mahea shared:

> Training from Baba Wekesa helped my practice to expand. It helped me to actively listen to the children because when you're doing the work, sometimes you're experiencing things that you really can't yet articulate. I didn't know why I felt certain things. Elders who have been doing this work for a longer period of time helped me to get further, faster. (M. Gaskins, personal communication, May 20, 2021)

More personally, a special bond was shared between Baba Wekesa and his wife Mama Afiya, which provided the Gaskins with courage when the work was lonely. Years later, Baba Wekesa, who works in Atlanta, Georgia, would fly to Alameda to lead the children in TVM in deep study of their cultural lineage. His presence was a dream come true for the Gaskins, who had yearned for this kind of exposure in their own childhoods. With Baba Wekesa, the

Gaskins manifested knowledge of self on a deeper level for the children of the village they cared for through the family lore project.

The Gaskins are clear that without ABEN, they are not sure when and how they would have connected with Baba Wekesa and the other powerful educators of its network. They are not sure who could have united the powerful work happening on the East coast with the West coast. For them, ABEN provided a critical connection for TVM.

Their Watering Hole: ABEN

The Gaskins refer to ABEN's Institutes as the watering hole, a place that brings together talented Black educators and leaders to share their knowledge, inspiration, and healing with the larger group. It is a place that, as Baba Asa Hilliard often shares, reawakens the African mind. Those who come believe their main responsibility is to nurture the genius of Black children who, in turn, have much to contribute to society. To the Gaskins, it is also a safe space to share joys, pains, successes, and failures. It is a place to be spiritually filled after the draining work of racial combat. Mahea and Mark stated:

> . . . we're not crazy. We're not isolated, there are other people who are just as angry or have just as strong a desire, if not stronger, to create spaces. And this is how they're doing it through their curriculum, through their networks, through their, you know, teaching series on Africa, all the different approaches that they had helped us to see. There's a network for us to plug into and come to as a watering hole of information resources. (M. Gaskins, personal communication, May 20, 2021)

Mahea observed how ABEN evolved over the years to embrace parents, teachers, community organizers, and curriculum writers, all educators in their own right. ABEN invites and includes all kinds of educators with diverse gifts and talents. Unlike other professional development models, Mahea noted that ABEN recognizes what can be created collectively when all voices are at the table. In return, the Gaskins received nourishment and inspiration from multiple perspectives and carried that back with them to Alameda, ready to implement change. Both note they may have eventually stumbled upon Chike Akua or Baba Wekesa but ABEN facilitated the process. Likewise, they pay it forward by sponsoring young educators so that they can attend the ABEN Institute. The young educators shared back with them comments like, "We never knew all of this existed [for Black children]!" In retrospect, Mark shares the following thoughts about ABEN:

> [ABEN] is like a really good concert where you feel connected! You find yourself really reactive . . . ABEN helps you to think about how to be more proactive—to be in planning posture. (M. Gaskins, personal communication, May 20, 2021)

Mahea reflected:

> ABEN is like a garden, the seeds are planted when one goes to ABEN and everyone takes, and then sometimes the seeds are blown off and shared . . . those who eat have been blessed. (M. Gaskins, personal communication, May 20, 2021)

Their work has not been easy. To be sure, TVM offers a counternarrative to the destructive forces in education in the United States and the Gaskins have met much resistance. Over the years, they have worked around obstructionists, through the "side door," and in spaces outside the school district to share messaging with parents and to create systems that serve Black children. For the Gaskins, ABEN offered much needed support, even if it was just to hear "we got you." They know that there is a special place where people are doing the work, and they feel connected.

Questions

Discuss ways that you have sought to grow or strengthen your professional networks. How did you find your tribe? What resources are available in your community to support your work with Black children?

References

Somé, M. P. (1998). *The healing wisdom of Africa: Finding life purpose through nature, ritual, and community* (1st ed.). J.P. Tarcher/Putnam.

Union City. (n.d.). Retrieved December 12, 2022, from https://www.unioncity.org/150/About-Union-City

SEVEN

From National to International Reach: The Sankofa Homeschool Collective

Monica Z. Utsey-Okpoti

"You have to meet her," said my good friend, Kyna Clemons. "She is amazing. The work she is doing for the community is life-changing." We had many conversations about this phenomenal woman she had been working with and Kyna was determined for us to meet and we did. During a brief stop in Washington, DC, on the way back to California, this great woman, Debra Watkins, made plans for us to meet for dinner at a Ghanaian restaurant in the Adams Morgan neighborhood of Washington, D.C. The meeting place was perfect because I had just returned from Ghana and I was craving Ghanaian food! When we met, it was like being around an old friend. We talked about Ghana and our work ensuring the success of Black children. We vowed to stay in contact. Little did we know at that time that a global pandemic would bring us back together again.

I had just returned from my third trip to Ghana when I started reading reports about a virus that was wreaking havoc on the people of China. I did not pay much attention to what was happening with the new virus until I heard that someone in Virginia had been infected. I remember thinking that Virginia was a little too close for comfort. Then came the notice slipped under my door by the rental office. Someone in my apartment had tested positive for COVID-19. I thought, "Oh my God!" Now I was finally paying attention to what was happening! I went to work on Monday and my principal called an emergency meeting. The principal said that the school building would be shut until further notice and that staff would be working from home. It all happened so fast. I had literally just returned to the United States and apparently, I missed being locked down in Ghana by a split second. Sadly, I had friends who had been traveling in Ghana who were stuck there for close to 4 months. An Instagram friend of mine got stuck and decided to never return to the United States. He is still there.

At first, working from home and not having to go anywhere was wonderful. I loved having everyone at home working virtually. We were one big happy, virtual family. I was enjoying the new normal until the public schools shut down. Then I got a call from Debra Watkins. What were we going to do!? My break did not last long; as educators, we feel responsible. Children were being sent home from school en masse with nothing more than a homework packet, and some students were not even given homework packets. Parents were distraught and feeling hopeless as they had entrusted the school system to educate their children, but now they were on their own. Homeschoolers, on the other hand, were in a much better situation. We resumed business as usual. We had always been responsible for our children's education. In many ways, we saw COVID-19 as a wrinkle that barely affected us. But homeschoolers could not continue to educate in our bubble while the rest of the children of the community languished. Debra Watkins (aka Mama Debra) was certainly not going to allow children in California or the nation to fall by the wayside. It was during that time that the ABEN and Sankofa homeschool collective partnership came into being. Mama Debra reached out to me on behalf of stressed out parents. Most had never homeschooled before. Mama Debra entrusted me and the Sankofa homeschool community with making this unexpected emergency transition easier for parents to navigate. I became the homeschool liaison for ABEN, keeping the organization abreast of homeschool and educational opportunities for students to stay engaged while public schools worked on building virtual platforms. Although the Pandemic did not stop homeschools, we did have to cease having in-person classes.

I and several other moms founded the Sankofa Homeschool Collective in 2004. Our aim was to create a sacred community for our children as we walked an unfamiliar path. It was also a place where our children could come together and learn alongside their friends from instructors who looked like them and were passionate about their teaching from an African-centered perspective. We were thriving as a community. Our reputation was solid. We had our own little village on 34th Street in Mount Rainier. The children loved the classes, they loved lunchtime, and they loved socializing even more. We supported the businesses in the Mount Rainier, Maryland community, so it was a win-win. The Pandemic turned the lights out for the collective. Prior to COVID-19, Sankofa Homeschool Collective was a 100% in-person educational enrichment program. Our core mission was to build community through relationships and that was supported through in-person learning. Now that we were unable to meet in person, I, along with Jessica Silva, my codirector and partner for the Sankofa Homeschool Collective, decided to just wait it out. That all changed when I was approached by Mama Debra who asked whether Sankofa offered online classes.

Although we had discussed online classes prior to her inquiry, and we had attempted some version of it when we did a Facebook livestream of our classes free of charge to a small homeschooling group in Trinidad, unfortunately it only lasted one semester. We were not able to use direct instruction, and the students in Trinidad were not engaged or able to fully participate. But our second attempt was different. We reasoned that if the school systems could pull an online program out of thin air, the least we could do was give it a try. I responded affirmatively to Mama Debra. And so, the whirlwind began of choosing classes, marketing classes, and training our teachers how to use an online platform. I was hired by Mama Debra to work with ABEN to be a direct liaison for parents who were suddenly homeschooling in California and across the nation, and that task changed the trajectory for the Sankofa Homeschool Collective.

My partner, Jessica Silva, and I went to work coordinating the classes, getting teachers on board with virtual learning, and training them on how to use Zoom and Google Classroom. Through ABEN, Mama Debra and her extensive educational network marketed that there was a culturally affirming alternative available for children and families who had been left with next to nothing because of the Pandemic. In the spring of 2020, the Sankofa Homeschool Collective held its first virtual session. Our enrollment tripled. We had students enrolled from all over the country and the world. Many were public school students whose school district had done very little to keep students engaged during the Pandemic.

We had time zones all over the place—East Coast, West Coast and even GMT with students in Ghana and Nigeria. It was an exciting juggle and deeply gratifying service. There were many parents who discovered that homeschooling was something they would continue once schools reopened. One of my favorite stories is of a parent whose teenage son had very little interest in traditional school. He was enrolled in the Grassroots Journalism class. In this course, youth learned to navigate the storytelling process and contributed to an anthology of articles about people, places, and objects relevant to their lives and that of their peers. When the instructor had to cancel the class, his mom told us he asked, "Why?" Now this may not seem like much, but to his mother it was monumental that he even cared. She said he asked twice. We later learned that her son truly enjoyed the class. Male instructors are rare and engaging in subject matter that is culturally relevant with an aim to uplift our people is even rarer in a public school setting.

Thanks to Debra Watkins and the ABEN network, Sankofa Homeschool Collective had gone from a very well-regarded, largely DC/Maryland/Virginia (DMV)-known program to one that families and children now had access to worldwide. Sankofa students from the DMV now had classes with public and private school students from Philadelphia, California, New Jersey, Ghana, and Nigeria.

Prior to the Pandemic, Sankofa Homeschool Collective had been held at a number of locations. We started out at the Deanwood Recreation Center in Northeast Washington, DC, followed by the Adinkra Cultural Arts Studios, and finally, the Fort Chaplin Apartments Community Center. Finding space in the city was extremely difficult. Most homeschool collectives in Maryland and Virginia are held in churches. We aimed to keep our program in DC and near a Metro bus or train stop to keep it accessible to as many families as possible, and that was a struggle. Virtual classes eliminated the need to search for space. Virtual classes also allowed us to offer more classes for each age group. Through our partnership with ABEN, Sankofa homeschool collective was able to expand its reach farther than ever before. Once schools reopened, we erred on the side of caution and continued with our virtual program, only now we were offering almost 25 classes! That is double what we were able to offer in the past. We hope to expand the program even more to reach more families.

In addition to influencing the virtual birth of the Sankofa Homeschool Collective online classes, Mama Debra planted another seed: virtual tours to Africa. I visited Ghana for the first time in 2019 during the historic "Year of Return." My sons, Zion and Ayinde, are both members of Farafina Kan, which is a West African drum ensemble based in DC. They were going to Africa to perform. Sankofa Homeschool Collective is an African-centered program so travel to Africa was a big part of the dreams and goals for our families. I had no idea I would be one of the first to go. After the first trip, I fell in love with Ghana and returned several times. I began a partnership with HIM Tours Ghana, an Accra-based tourism company. When the Pandemic hit, tourism was devastated. Not only was the United States on lockdown, but many parts of the world were as well. But being on lockdown in Ghana was far different from being on lockdown in the United States. In Ghana, there were no creature comforts for people who are a part of an informal economy that has to get out there and hustle for their daily bread. Because I shared so many of my Ghana adventure videos on social media, Mama Debra thought that sharing those kinds of adventures may be beneficial for children who were yanked out of school and had their worlds turned upside down.

I was a part of the planning team for both virtual tours to Ghana. I was the liaison with HIM Tours in Ghana. For tourism professionals who were on lockdown and travelers who were locked out, the virtual tour idea was a godsend. This idea fed both sides of the Atlantic. The souls of children were fed in the United States and children were literally fed in Ghana due to tour guides having worked during a Pandemic. Daniel Okoe Okpoti, the founder of HIM Tours Ghana, was our lifeline. This was a tall ask during a Pandemic because he operated a small company and access to technology can be challenging. He worked hard to make it happen. Virtual tours were unheard of to many of the guides at the historic sites that Brother Daniel approached, but they were certainly not turning business down. After months of preparation, students traveled to Ghana in July of 2021 from their private homes and experienced historic Jamestown, Kwame Nkrumah Park, Cape Coast Dungeons, the Center for Cultural Arts, and shopping at Makola Market. Students also visited the Western Region of Ghana, which is seven hours from Accra, to see Nzulezu, a village built entirely on stilts in the middle of a lake. This kind of tour of Africa is something that many of the children on the tour may not ever be able to afford to see in person. The virtual tours placed something special into the hearts and minds of the children.

The first virtual tour was so successful that there was a high demand to do it again. So, we went back to the drawing board. HIM Tours led the way again. This time, students virtually visited Kumasi in the Ashanti Region. They saw Bonwire, where Kente cloth is woven, and visited Kejetia, the largest open-air market in all of West Africa. They traced their stolen ancestors' steps from their last bath at Assin Manso before being ripped away from mother Africa. Many myths about Africa were put to rest and many questions about Africa were answered. Additionally, with all that I learned while working with ABEN, I was able to host a third virtual tour for Sankofa Homeschool Collective specifically. Obi Egbuna, Jr., our Pan-African History teacher, led the discussion. Students who have been learning with him for years know the story of Osagyefo Dr. Kwame Nkrumah, the visionary leader who ushered Ghana into its independence from colonial rule. This virtual tour was a visual way for students to see that history is alive.

The Sankofa Homeschool Collective partnership with ABEN continues. Their vision and mission are in perfect alignment with Sankofa. Educators around the country are blessed that an organization such as ABEN exists, one that educates the educators in all things Black, all things culturally uplifting and, in all things, Black excellence. I look forward to future endeavors, ones that allow educators who really love our children, to survive both financially and professionally. ABEN supports organizations by giving them the motivational and financial wings to fly. We have been able to bless others through ABEN's blessing and for that, the Sankofa Homeschool Collective is forever grateful.

Questions

Debra Watkins pivoted quickly during the Pandemic to partner with an organization to create online "master classes" that were culturally centered for Black youth in the United States and abroad. What are ways you or your organization have had to pivot to stay timely?

PART III

PERSONAL NARRATIVES OF SOUL-CENTERED HEALING

EIGHT

Leading Outside of the White Gaze: Debra Watkins, Founder of ABEN

Rona M. Frederick, PhD

MASTER TEACHER BABA T'SHANGO MBILISHAKA uses the following metaphor originated by Wade Boykin to describe three types of students: The student that is the Rock doesn't do anything—you might find him in the corner. The Sponge soaks up information and can regurgitate back, but he is not a thinker. The Spark is the one that goes above and beyond and does additional research. The Spark will sit in the front of the classroom and question the teacher. He might create his own original proverb after hearing others. Baba T'shango would say that the spark is what we need in the African community!

Debra Watkins is a spark that created a fire. She shares that she was born with a flame in her belly and an intense love for African people. She serves as the founder and executive director of A Black Education Network (ABEN), an outgrowth of the California Alliance of African American Educators (CAAAE). Over the past 20 years, she has raised millions of dollars to support Black-led programming, culturally responsive resources, and grassroots organizations. In fact, she sees it as her moral obligation to support the "good works in the community" especially because Black-led organizations receive the least amount of philanthropic financial support, less than any other race, for their endeavors (Atkins & Aguilar, 2012). She has poured resources into thousands of young people, families, and community organizers.

Debra Watkins sees herself as a teacher-activist changing the trajectory from negative to positive for Black youth. Using her skills and talents to organize and strategize, she finds ways to push the needle toward Black liberation. In addition to building Black-led, self-sustaining institutions, she stands in solidarity with any cause that is aligned with her commitment to improving the lives of Black children.

Those who work directly with Debra Watkins and those who admire her from afar, would describe her as a fiery, feisty, blunt, unrelenting warrior who will defend the honor of Black children, at times without regard for financial gain. One grassroots organizer, Mark Gaskins, described her as "a punch in the mouth for those who work against the liberation of Black children." Unapologetically Black, she lives and breathes Black excellence, not only in her pedagogy as a Master teacher but also as a leader, organizer, and institution builder. Her leadership and her impact also manifest in the ways she cares for others.

Debra Watkins can be considered as what Ware (2006) refers to as a "warm demander." Used in the teaching realm, a warm demander refers to an educator who communicates love and warmth toward students while demanding that they work toward high standards. She smiles as she says she might consider herself "50% warm and 50% demanding." As a trained counselor, her warm side includes being an active listener and an engaging conversationalist. She is affirming and cares deeply about her relationships. Debra's impeccable knack for recognizing the spiritual gifts and talents that people bring to the table enables her to help others tap into their gifts at the right time and for the right reason. She is a connector who knows both how to build alliances and to not burn bridges even when she is disappointed by the outcome. Debra unconditionally and patiently supports young organizers who desire her jegnaship and, Gloria Rosaline Preudhomme shared that as a community organizer, she has been known to always have a room available and food to eat for anyone who needs a home away from home. Most importantly, she is committed to passing the torch to the next generation who will carry on the intergenerational legacy of excellence for the Black community.

Debra's demanding side shows up in the high expectations she sets for those with whom she works. Admittedly a driver, she holds others accountable and will not permit excuses or coddling for her Black allies and those for which she serves as a jegna. Whereas many who work with her are compelled by her unrelenting love and passion for Black children, others are unable to withstand the pressure, and some may even leave. Debra Watkins is a formidable opponent against anyone who dares to break the spirit of Black children. In fact, she has been known to publicly call out folks if they move in a direction she believes is not right. Debra's goal is to show results and she will not tolerate failure.

The warrior/activist would readily admit that the work of racial uplift can be daunting, especially when so many have no will to try. Having watched her brother fall victim to the racialized terror experienced by many youth in the United States, Debra believes much needs to be done. Her vehicle of choice is education, and she works both within and outside existing systems to support Black children and families. Her ultimate dream is 1,000 self-sustaining schools that epitomize Black excellence in pedagogy, curriculum, and community engagement. She is determined to identify and persuade a funder to invest $1 million a year for 10 years for the national design of a Black school system. Many who know Debra Watkins believe it is not a question of if, but when her goal will come to fruition.

A Unique Set of Skills

Debra Watkins developed a unique skill set through her teaching and organizing career. Her life is framed by her positionality of being a Black, female, middle class, mother, and grandmother living in a racist country. Like Harriet Tubman, Sojourner Truth, and Ella Baker, she embodies her role as warrior, protector, connector, and nurturer, not only for her biological child, but for all Black children. Othermothering, in the words of Patricia Hill Collins (2009), underscores her work as both a teacher and a leader. Having married a tech engineer in Silicon Valley during the dot-com rise, she has experienced some aspects of poverty (as a child) and wealth (as a wife and mother), which inform her uniquely empathetic stance. She has also "sat at the foot" of influential African-centered elders like Barbara Sizemore, Asa Hilliard, Joyce King, and Wade Nobles, all of whom have deeply informed her African ideology and psyche on the importance of Sankofa—returning to the African source. Shockley refers to this as "cultural reattachment" (Shockley & Frederick, 2010):

> The lessons learned by Afrocentric educationists such as Akoto and Anwisye, both of whom are school leaders and researchers, include the dire need for Blacks to reattach to African culture for the purposes of family and community building (Anwisye, 2006). Although African culture is understood as nonstatic, the traditional practices of continental Africans are viewed as proper cultural examples for people of African descent. Akoto and Akoto (1999) illuminated three broad overlapping stages of re-Africanization (rediscovery/historical recovery, redefinition/cultural reaffirmation, and revitalization/national liberation) that undergird the curricular focus of Afrocentric schools. The three

> stages indicate crucial aspects of what is considered to be a return to African cultural practice. (p. 1223)

Debra Watkins embraces historical recovery, national liberation, and cultural reaffirmation. She believes in the global rallying cry "We are an African people." She readily embraces her role as healer, political organizer, protector of the children, retainer of culture, and life affirmer (Gallman et al., 2003, p. 42). Through her institution-building, she holds the space for both youth and elders, and accepts the calling to transmit intergenerational knowledge. Her programming exemplifies the highest standards of achievement in the areas of science, technology, engineering, and math (STEM), demonstrating a deep respect for the achievements of African giants such as the ancient multigenius Imhotep, and tapping into the natural genius of children, thereby demonstrating her commitment to the survival of African people. As a consummate reader, she is well-informed of the current trends and trailblazers in education. She brings forth historical memory from the past and embraces the brilliance of young scholars and activists who are the future.

Debra Watkins is proud of her work in helping to build four thriving organizations—Santa Clara County Alliance of Black Educators, CAAAE/ ABEN, Greene Scholars, Black Students of California United (BSCU)—all of which serve Black youth. Her adept fundraising and grant-writing skills have ensured healthy budgets for each of the organizations and have enabled her to support many other Black-led initiatives, including Anthony Browder's ASA Restoration Project, Children of the Sun African-centered curriculum writing, and the Sankofa Homeschool Collective. What was once a networking and professional development initiative dedicated to Black excellence (CAAAE) has become a national mechanism for change that promotes the achievement of Black academic and cultural excellence (ACE) through schools, school districts, education funders, nonprofits/community-based organizations, local and state government, higher education institutions, think tanks, educator unions and associations.

Debra Watkins' ultimate goal is clear; to combat the psychological damage and trauma that has become normalized within the U.S. school system. First, she seeks to transform the public narratives about the history and accomplishments of Black students who are often framed as deficient, nonachieving, and lazy. Knowledge of self and one's history prior to enslavement is of utmost importance. Accordingly, Debra Watkins engages parents and family members in the process of learning more about their individual histories and cultures, and also provides academic and cultural enrichment programs and services to students within and outside school settings to foster greater cultural and historic pride, and more positive identities.

My teachers poured into me!

Debra Watkins was born on July 25. At the age of 3, she lived in Compton, CA. She shared that, "my mom was a cook and my father was a janitor until they moved up the ranks and got better jobs. The best thing they did was to move us to Pomona in 1960 when I was just 7." Her parents moved Debra Watkins and her nine brothers and sisters to the suburbs "where they would have opportunities elusive to most Black children in America." In retrospect, she realizes that although those predominantly White schools were mediocre at best, they sheltered her from the substandard education most Black students were getting in "inner cities" across the country. Debra Watkins feels blessed to have moved from Watts to the "leafy suburbs" where her stepfather built a swing set and playhouse by hand in their backyard. She feels that she received opportunities and a decent education. Observing so many casualties of Black youth that suffered and even died due to the system, her personal motto remains "to whom much is given, much is required."

Debra Watkins felt protected while matriculating in the Pomona school system. Teachers recognized her brilliance and talent. She recognizes that even as a Black girl, she was among the favorites. She fondly remembers 4th grade when her teacher, Mr. Stevenson, said that she was the best writer in his class and that she should become an English teacher. It was at that moment that she set her sights on teaching and never looked back. She recalls, "He poured that into me and I said, 'OK.' And I love to read. I love to write. So it makes sense to me. I'll become an English teacher."

As she looks back on her experiences in school, Debra Watkins only remembers a few teachers. Those teachers, however, left a permanent mark. She recalls that they showed her the power of professionalism, and she holds memories of feeling special and of being the recipient of their kindness and care. What she remembers most is their passion for the art of teaching. She carried these attributes with her when she became a teacher years later.

High school offered the first opportunity for her to be exposed to Black literature. Although she doesn't remember the books, she remembers how the teaching made her feel, as well as how it felt to see herself represented in the literature. She shared in retrospect, "You know, I loved school. And from K to 12, I was a teacher's pet for most of my classes. And so that Eurocentric frame worked for me, it just didn't work for everybody." Former high school friends remember that she was always an organizer and race conscious. As a sophomore, she was one of the founders of the Black Student Union. She laughs as she recalls her experiences naming the club. In 1968, the administration was unwilling to allow the students to call the new organization the "Black Student Union" at the White high school. One of her Black peers, Jacques Bordeaux, consulted with his older brother and they named the new organization Amandla, a South African word for *power*. A year later, the administration allowed the name to change to the Soul Club and eventually, after Debra Watkins graduated, the name became the Black Student Union.

After graduating from high school, Debra Watkins was accepted into The American Field Service (AFS), a prestigious study abroad program. She lived with a host family for one year, attended the local lycée in what Americans would call 13th grade, became fluent in French, and earned the baccalaureate required of French students for admission to colleges and universities. The exposure to a world outside of Pomona was life-changing and instilled in her a love of travel and the knowledge that exposure to different cultures and experiences is vital for young people.

Unable to afford a 4-year college, Debra Watkins returned to the States and attended community college. She matriculated to Pitzer College, where she received a B.A. in English with minors in French and Psychology. As she looks back, she realized that her racialized consciousness was present at a young age. In 1975, while a junior in college, Debra Watkins recalls writing a research paper that critiqued integration. Similar to Derrick Bell, father of critical race theory, she shares:

> I knew that there was something inherently wrong with integration. And I grew up in a totally one hundred percent integrated place. When I say that I mean predominantly White schools, but they were all integrated. I wasn't bussed or anything and that was 1975 when busing was at its height in this country. (D. Watkins, personal communication, December 2, 2021)

She ponders reflectively and shares, "I wrote about the deleterious effects of integration. And here, Derrick Bell, around the same time period, was espousing the same views and I thought, 'Well, just fix the Black schools.' I knew nothing about systemic racism because I had not encountered it." Unbeknownst to her at the time, the burgeoning cultural theorist would spend her life doing just that—fixing Black schools and effectively reimagining education for Black youth.

Upon graduation from Pitzer in 1976, Debra Watkins matriculated into Stanford University's teacher education program to fulfill her dream of becoming a teacher. For the next 14 years, she taught in the East Side Union High School district of San Jose while raising her daughter. Independence High School in Santa Clara county opened in the fall of 1976. In the well-resourced high school, Debra Watkins felt she was extremely supported as a new teacher (Watkins, p. 44). She immediately connected with like-minded educators who cared deeply about the experiences of Black children. Recognizing the lack of self-knowledge and culturally responsive curriculum, she and a few colleagues founded the Black Student Union and served as advisors for the next 10 years. For Debra Watkins, the work of the organization was meaningful: The students learned about their Black history and "gain[ed] pride in being Black" (Watkins, p. 45).

As she taught, her critiques of the schools deepened. She noticed that most Black students were not "making it into her college-prep English course" (Watkins, p. 51). She observed real, systemic barriers that fueled disparity in access to gifted and specialized education.

The reality was both disturbing and disheartening. As a result, she became a founding member of the Santa Clara County Alliance of Black Educators, an affiliate of the National Alliance of Black School Educators (NABSE). In that role, the founders hosted annual back-to-school socials so local educators could network and listen to distinguished Black keynote speakers. Noticing that Black children were rarely recognized for their academic achievements, they also began the annual tradition of celebrating Black students transitioning from 5th, 6th, 8th or 12th grade (Watkins, p. 51). This organization would become the inspiration for CAAAE and later ABEN.

As Debra taught and organized, she became an avid student of the system. She watched the school's systemic practices that denied Black students access to high quality programming and advanced placement classes. She saw lowered expectations of Black youth. She observed that the Black students she taught had little to no knowledge of who they were culturally and no understanding of the power they held. She studied the institutional systems beyond schools as well, noticing how healthcare, policy, and community services supported systemic racism. She witnessed miseducation and its psychological impact on the youth. Almost 30 years later, she shared in retrospect, "When I think about systemic racism and its deliberate tactics to miseducate and disenfranchise, I am just glad that [I created] organizations designed to elevate Black students and their families, and I am still working at that." Because of this insight, one of her favorite quotes is by Haim Ginnot:

> I've come to a frightening conclusion that I am the decisive element in the classroom. It's my personal approach that creates the climate. It's my daily mood that makes the weather. As a teacher, I possess a tremendous power to make a child's life miserable or joyous. I can be a tool of torture or an instrument of inspiration. I can humiliate or heal. In all situations, it is my response that determines whether a crisis will be escalated or de-escalated, and a child humanized or dehumanized.
>
> —*Haim Ginott (1972)*

Philosophy

Debra Watkins owns her power and believes that she is the decisive element not only in the classroom but also within her spheres of influence. The above quote represents one of Debra Watkins' guiding principles. Every day she wakes up with clarity about the long-term impact of the *Ma'afa* (terror), the African Holocaust of enslavement, on the Black community generally and on Black children in particular. She recognizes that Black youth are under daily attack physically, mentally, and emotionally. Therefore, she owns the fact that it is up to her and the larger community to make a change.

She moves not out of reaction to colonization, enslavement, miseducation, racialized oppression, and trauma, but rather out of the sincere belief that it is necessary for African people to build a world, collectively, for future generations. To that end, she agrees with Hilliard that Black folks must self-determine their destiny and reclaim the minds of Afrikan youth (Gallman et al., p. 9). For Debra Watkins, process matters as much as outcome. In the same vein as Toussaint L'Ouverture, David Walker, Ella Baker, Harriet Tubman, Malcolm

X, Marcus Garvey, and others, she would ask, "How hard are you trying and what sincerity are you bringing to the mission of racial uplift and liberation for Black children?"

Her Jegnas: Kindred Spirits

Debra Watkins relies on like-minded allies, especially her jegnas, to help her accomplish her goals. She cites two people on whom she would bestow the title of jegna: Dr. Joyce King and Anthony Browder supported building her vision and African frames of references.

At the age of 48, Debra Watkins met Joyce King, former president of the American Educational Research Association and author of *Black Education: A Transformative Research and Action Agenda for the New Century* (2005). Debra Watkins fondly acknowledges that they share a special synergy and the same mission to uplift the Black community and Black children. She proudly pre-faces any mention of Dr. Joyce King with "my jegna, Dr. Joyce King."

Debra Watkins initially met King when King served as director for the teacher education program at Santa Clara University. Via a cold call, she asked King to serve as a panelist to judge the model schools her students designed. They reconnected in 2002, years later, through Susan Taylor (former long-time editor of *Essence* magazine) and, in 2007, when Dr. Wade Nobles, a renowned psychologist, recommended King as a keynote speaker for the 5th annual CAAAE Institute. Debra was riveted by King's presentation and brilliance and immediately asked her to serve on CAAAE's advisory board.

Debra describes King as "the wind beneath my wings." She gets the money, and King helps her to envision the plan. Debra Watkins also credits King for deepening her understanding of African-centered education and practice. She shared that although she had a deep understanding of systemic racism and White supremacy, it was King who helped her to create a conceptual framework around how "this [race and an African-centered consciousness] all sort of hung together . . . it was almost like baptism by fire." Debra Watkins attended lectures and read. She traveled to Accra, Ghana in 2000 with Dr. Nobles and Dr. Na'im Akbar and has been there two other times as well as to South Africa (twice), Nigeria, and Egypt.

Dr. Joyce King gave Debra Watkins her entree into the world of academia by sharing with her the challenges of being Black and of working in higher education. As a result, ABEN centered the voices of academics along with teachers, administrators, parents, and grassroot organizers at its annual Summer Institutes held at Stanford University's Graduate School of Education. However, Debra Watkins credits Dr. King for pushing her in other ways. Dr. King and Debra Watkins would push each other. We always say to each other, "Girl, we did some powerful stuff!"

Likewise, Anthony Browder, with whom she fondly refers to as Mr. Browder, also deepened her African consciousness. A few months after he keynoted at the October 2013 Black Education Congress that Debra Watkins helped coordinate with the support of Dr. King and Dr. Iva Carruthers, they became business partners and visionaries in the fight for Black children. Debra shares that over the years Mr. Browder has helped her navigate the African-centered world. More than that, he is unapologetically African.

On Being a Pioneer, Leader, and Philanthropist

Envisioning

Everyone has their part to play in the liberation of Black children. Debra Watkins is clear on her role and responsibilities. She states emphatically that she "stays in her lane" as a visionary, funder, educator, and a connector. She also recognizes that no one does the kind of work she does using her skill sets as an educator and a funder to reach, educate, and transform the minds and psyches of Black children and the Black community. In communities across California and the country, what began as a space for connecting educators to best practices in Black education has become a systems-change model rooted in Nguzo Saba, the seven core principles of Kwanzaa; unity (umoja), self-determination (kujichagulia), collective responsibility (ujima), cooperative economics (ujamaa), purpose (nia), creativity (kuumba) and faith (imani).

The power of the CAAAE/ABEN Institutes is widely recognized. Debra Watkins understood, in the '90s, that the development of Black educators in the United States required a different mindset and thought pattern that could not be learned in traditional White university or alternative teacher preparation programs. This thought pattern, grounded in an African worldview, begins with the belief that the brilliant African child is the foundation of the society and determines the quality of its community (Fu-Kiau & Lukondo-Wamba,

2000). Education, and therefore pedagogy, is a socializing process, and the destiny of the community is tied together with all members, from ancestors to those not yet born. In the words of Hilliard (as cited in Gallman et al., 2003):

> African teachers recognize the genius and the divinity of each of our children, speaking to and teaching to each child's intellect, humanity, and spirit. . . . African teachers recognize the centrality of relationships between teachers and students, among students and within the African community as a whole. (p. 63)

It was Debra Watkins' vision to make that knowledge available to the masses. At the time, simply hearing Black researchers provide instruction on evidence-based best practices for Black children was novel. Attendees at the Institutes would share that they did not know research for Black children existed.

However, over time, the ABEN Institutes and annual membership breakfasts became a space for educators, policymakers, parents, and organizers striving to foster spaces of academic excellence in their home communities to be "fed and healed" by members of their "tribe." Going to the Institutes, hearing dynamic speakers. and leaving the forum with a sound action plan and materials to support their local communities was the intended goal. As evidenced by participant feedback, attendees left the Institutes feeling "connected and charged." Attendees also shared that the Institutes allowed their souls to be fed and nourished for the hard work ahead. This simple act is important to Debra Watkins, who says, "I honor people's time; I value their presence; I care about who they are and what they bring to the table."

"I am a Connector!"

In many ways Debra Watkins shows up as what Horsford and Tillman (2013) call a "bridge leader." They argue that bridge leadership is historically practiced by Black women leaders who fight for both equality and social justice framed through their unique positionality and lens. The term is used to describe "how the intersection of race and gender as experienced by [a] Black woman has resulted in her serving as a bridge for others, to others, and between others in oppressive and discriminatory contexts over time" (Horsford, S.D., & Tillman, L.C., 2013, p. 18). As a Black woman committed to the liberation of her race, Debra Watkins serves as connector, a bridge. Her

Institutes and African-centered programming connect practitioners with best practices in Black education, and her philanthropic efforts financially support numerous Black organizations.

What makes her bridge approach remarkable is that, unlike many Black Americans who need to mask their real selves to navigate in U.S. systems, at times for reasons of safety and security, Debra Watkins carries her African identity into the boardroom of various organizations, to school districts, and to her funders—everyone is clear on her mission. She is unwilling to accept social arrangements that limit Black children and that restrict them from deeply understanding their relationship to their African selves. Although she pragmatically and eloquently speaks the language of "evidence-based practice," "logic models," and "impact through research," in the final analysis, she is clear: if funders don't accept her mission toward Black liberation, she is uninterested in their money. For those that become allies, she is more than willing to work with them.

Debra Watkins also bridges relationships. Much of her downtime is spent seeking out those freedom fighters who are doing the work on the ground across the nation. She studies, reads, and listens for community endeavors that are making a difference for Black children. Whether through a cold call or an outreach email, she finds opportunities to connect and share the work of ABEN. It is not uncommon for the connection to become an ongoing relationship, which is a source of pride for Debra Watkins. She serves as jegna to community organizers and young scholars. In essence, she invests time and resources to build an army of those who are committed to Black liberation within and outside the system.

Bridging also presents itself through her intentional focus on intergenerational connections. She makes it a point at every Institute to include the voices of both youth and elders. Serving as sages, the elders restore the cultural memory and gently add constructive feedback to support the work of the youth.

In addition, Debra Watkins' organizations bridge Black children all over the nation to academic excellence and reattaching them to their culture in their hometowns through the action-oriented mission of the Institutes and programming, such as Cultural Imperative Initiative, Greene Scholars, and virtual tours to Ghana, Nigeria, and Kenya.

Philanthropy

Philanthropy has become a vital part of Debra Watkins' tool kit. In fact, her eyes light up when she reflects on the difference she is making in communities through the funds she provides. Some would argue it is the most important part of her work. She funds endeavors that are changing the lives of Black children.

Debra Watkins has no problem relying heavily on non-Black benefactors to fund her organization. Her unique stance on reparations fuels her drive to raise money from non-Black funders. She shares, "Getting funding from White people is one form of reparations because this country's vast wealth comes in large part from the free labor of our African ancestors. We are here to pick up and cash those checks that they were never given."

Her only regret is that more wealthy Blacks don't fund her projects. In spite of utilizing non-Black money, ABEN is 100% Black-led and Black-run. She recruits people of African ancestry to serve on her board, and she does not have non-Black team members. To be clear, she does not hire Blacks for the sake of Blackness. Those who are placed on the board or hired as team members respect and at times embody an African-centered philosophy. They utilize the Nguzo Saba principles as a guiding force for their work and are experts in their craft.

The Debra Magic

Folks often speak of the Debra Magic. It is not uncommon for folks to say "the Institute was magical and so professional!" or "Debra makes resources just appear." Indeed, she has raised millions of dollars to support Black-led initiatives that serve Black educators and children, but there is no "magic" involved. Her steps are measured, intentional, strategic, and well planned, and they reflect her years of fine-tuned experience and laser-like focus. Most importantly, she thinks big.

"Oh, I Just Picked up the Phone and Called"

Debra Watkins moves with a fierce boldness when it comes to garnering money and resources for Black children. When first starting the Carver Scholars

Program (CSP), the STEM precursor to the Greene Scholars program, she attended a panel focused on diversifying the STEM pipeline in Silicon Valley. The panel consisted of major players in the tech industry including the dean of the Engineering Department at UC Davis and Dr. T. J. Rodgers, founder and CEO of Cypress Semiconductor. During the question-and-answer portion, Watkins went to the microphone and announced that she had just received her first $50,000 from Intel. She continued to add that if any company representatives were really interested in diversifying the workforce, she would be in the back of the room and would be happy to speak with them. After the session, a hearty line of funders gathered to discuss how they could partner with her organization.

Rarely does Debra miss an opportunity to promote her organizations. After she finished speaking to the funders in her line, she hopped in Dr. T.J. Rodgers' line to share a bit more about CSP. He remembered her announcement about the money she received from Intel and told her on the spot that his company would donate $25,000. Within two weeks, the check was in the organization's bank account.

"Just asking" also worked to Debra Watkins' advantage when she went back to her most consistent donor, Dr. T.J. Rodgers, for more resources. As a result of her ask, seven years later, the then newly-formed Greene Scholars program (GSP) attained a lab with 30 computers as well as office and conference space at the Cypress headquarters. When Cypress needed the lab a few years later, Dr. Rodgers agreed to the relocation of GSP elsewhere on his company's campus as long as the space was better than what the program had previously. The GSP was given access to the entire first floor of Cypress' headquarters as well as office cubicles on the third floor. This unprecedented access to prime Silicon Valley real estate was granted for 14 years until COVID-19 hit. After conducting the GSP virtually for 18 months during the Pandemic, Cypress agreed to donate $50,000 annually to cover rental needs for the GSP.

Debra's boldness in "just asking" also landed a home for the CAAAE/ABEN Institutes and gained the organization's solid supporter in Dr. Linda Darling-Hammond and a wisdom circle with some of the most sought-after Black researchers in the field. Debra Watkins never forgets a conversation and seeks opportunities to build relationships that are mutually beneficial. When seeking board members, she recalled a brief conversation at a meeting in Sacramento for the statewide National Board Certification committee of which she was a member. She struck up a conversation with Anne Ifekwunigwe, an elementary school teacher who was running a center at UCLA to increase the number of Black teachers who would become Board certified, one of the most rigorous teacher evaluation systems in the country. Debra Watkins shared that Anne's brilliance left an impression. She did not hesitate to ask her on the spot to become the CAAAE coordinator for the Los Angeles region. Anne accepted.

"Build Alliances – This is One of the Most Critical Pieces to the Success of my Institution"

Debra Watkins recognizes the brilliance of those around her. She moves with and on purpose (Nia). She has an uncanny ability to utilize their gifts and talents in ways that move her organization. At the same time, she values relationships and cares deeply about those who are in her world.

Debra Watkins believes in a "big tent" philosophy. Her desire is to reimagine African-centered education in a way that is inclusive of the masses. She recognizes that not everyone shares that ethos. For ABEN, however, everyone is invited to partake, from administrators, teachers, community members, or academics to anywhere on the spectrum from African-centered to race-conscious to even those who are in the process of becoming. She is guided by a belief that everyone has something to contribute, everyone is heard, and everyone will go back to their community and make change.

As such, Debra strives to connect and work with like-minded warriors. Her army includes African-centered curriculum writers; grassroots organizers who sponsor culturally responsive African-centered programs; and academics, who, in clandestine spaces, strategically outline a national liberatory plan for Black children. It is not uncommon for Debra to hear or read about the good works of an organization and ask a friend or colleague to connect the two for conversations including invitations to join the ABEN network or for donating financial support. Debra Watkins has been known to support any and all causes here and abroad that educate, heal, and protect African children. ABEN serves as her vehicle to do just that.

"I Broke the Code!" – On Fundraising

Over the years, Debra Watkins has mastered grant writing. She shares, "I'm an English major so I took a grant writing class from the Foundation Center. Writing comes easily to me." She also recognizes that years of evidenced-based practice and a record of successful grant cycles has catapulted ABEN to a level of fundraising success.

Years of strategically building out her network uniquely positioned her to be exposed to the wealthiest foundations. She is an avid reader of the *Chronicle of Philanthropy* and holds professional memberships in ABFE, A Philanthropic Partnership for Black Communities, and the National Committee for Responsive Philanthropy (NCRP). Debra Watkins has researched the major players' roles and responsibilities and positioned herself in ways that would allow for meaningful connections. Clarity around her elevator pitch and evidence of results all came together to ensure the highest quality of interaction and relationship building. Her every move is calculated. Weekly hour-long one-on-one meetings with her leadership team allow her to closely monitor the inner workings of ABEN. Debra Watkins also deeply understands the value of evidence-based results and high-quality programming. Research, evaluation, and programmatic replication are all tools in her wheelhouse.

Debra Watkins feels a sense of sadness when she hears Black leaders express overwhelming appreciation for what she considers a small gift of $10,000. At one point, she would have agreed that $10,000 was huge; however, years of closely studying and being a part of the philanthropic world has taught her that non-Black organizations garner millions yearly and that Black organizations garner the tiniest piece of the pie. She desires to do more and to give more.

Reimagining Outside of the White Gaze

The current political terrain and state of Black education requires Black leaders to reimagine. Debra Watkins has blessed hundreds of Black community members and nonprofits with monetary gifts simply because of their good deeds in the community. One academic shared, "Oh I know Debra Watkins. She gave the documentary $500 after I met her at a conference." Another Vice Principal of a school shared that after meeting Debra Watkins, Watkins helped her write a proposal for a STEM grant. About this Debra Watkins says, "I broke the code. I didn't have anybody trailblazing, raising money for me . . . but I'm paying it forward because I'm thinking, 'I've learned so much. I have much to give.'"

Debra Watkins is clear and focused. Money sustains the grassroots work in the community and has a direct impact on the lives of Black children. And she ensures that the resources reach the communities of Black children most in need. She emphatically states, "It is not enough to fight anti-Blackness, we must be pro-Black!"

Toni Morrison, one of Debra Watkins' favorite writers, was critiqued for not juxtaposing the lives of Black people with Whites. To this Morrison replied, "I have spent my entire writing life trying to make sure that the White gaze was not the dominant one in any of my books." Debra Watkins agrees. With her eyes on the prize, she spends her lifetime ensuring that her gaze is directed at self-knowledge, cultural empowerment, and sovereignty for the Black community.

Questions

Common ways of thinking about leadership are adoptive, transformative, liberatory etc. Think about Debra Watkins' leadership as a case. Discuss her leadership style and illustrations. How would you define her leadership?

References

Atkins, A., & Aguilar, O. (2012). *A promise to diverse communities: Summary of foundation coalition's efforts*. The Greenlining Institute.

Fu-Kiau, K., & Lukondo-Wamba, A. (2000). *Kindezi: The Kãongo art of babysitting*. Imprint Editions.

Gallman, B. K., Williams, L. O., & Ani, M. W. (2003). *To be Afrikan: Essays by Afrikans in the process of Sankofa (Returning to our source of power)*. Maat.

Ginott, H. (1972). Teacher and child: A book for parents and teachers. McMillan.

Hill Collins, P. (2009). *Black feminist thought: Knowledge, consciousness, and the politics of empowerment* (2nd ed.). Routledge.

Horsford, S. D., & Tillman, L. C. (2013). *Intersectional identities and educational leadership of Black women in the USA*. Routledge.

King, J. E. (Ed.). (2005). *Black education: A transformative research and action agenda for the new century*. Routledge.

Nobles, W. W. (1986). *African psychology: Toward its reclamation, reascension and revitalization.* Black Family Institute.

Shockley, K. G., & Frederick, R. M. (2010). Constructs and dimensions of Afrocentric education. *Journal of Black Studies, 40*(6), 1212–1233. https://doi.org/10.1177/0021934708325517

Ware, F. (2006). Warm demander pedagogy: Culturally responsive teaching that supports a culture of achievement for African American students. *Urban Education, 41*(4), 427–456. https://doi.org/10.1177/0042085906289710

Watkins, D. (2016). *Thoughts held hostage: A Black teachers journey to unlocking young minds.* ABEN.

NINE

ABEN: A Lighthouse

Rev. Akosua Lesesne, EdD

In my childhood home, my intelligence was celebrated—egged on really—and Black women led. All of them were dark-skinned like me. This was not the case once I began school. From Kindergarten through the 12th grade, I had 38 teachers; only three of them were Black. In the eyes of many, I have succeeded both academically and professionally. It's more accurate to say I survived and at times thrived because of the love and pedagogical genius I received at home *despite* my educational experiences, not because of them. Being educated in White-governed and White-dominated spaces led to an unbroken string of racial traumas. This success came at a great cost to my psyche and my soul. I experienced a great deal of isolation and soul-corrosive racial harm throughout my educational journey. When I became a teacher, then district leader, educational design leader, doctoral student, and eventually founded two educational organizations, the othering I experienced and psychic racial violence only seemed to heighten with my ascension into these spaces. I also experienced a distinctive connection among my Black students, their parents, communities and me. True to the anti-Black culture I described, however, the liberatory ideas I proposed based on these relationships were often dismissed by the White establishment. That was the case despite generations of Black teaching excellence documented by practice, oral history research, and recent studies showing that Black teachers have a distinctively more positive impact on Black school children's well-being and academic success (Delpit, 2006; View et al., 2019) .

The higher I ascended into the ranks, the more racial trauma I experienced until this trauma turned into terror at the normalized anti-Blackness among White (and some Black) people who have so much control over the educational lives of Black children. I doubled down and clung even more closely to the lighthouses and anchors of these rich legacies of Black teaching excellence as I've navigated this sea of anti-Blackness in honor of my calling as a Black educator and for the love, liberation, and genius of Black children. Debra

Watkins' work through ABEN has been one of those lighthouses. Debra Watkins herself has been one of these anchors.

Prior to 2018, ABEN's work was a lighthouse far off in the distance in California while I was on the East Coast. Witnessing ABEN's work from afar was affirming and encouraging. It was obvious ABEN centered Black children and their limitless capabilities. ABEN also relied solely on the deep and rich body of knowledge and practice produced by and for Black people. This approach was in stark contrast to what I was experiencing in the spaces in which I worked. One of the most insidious aspects of the tyranny of Whiteness in Black education is the utter disregard for the proven practices, ideas, values, and scholarship of Black people. I worked in horror as entire so-called educational reform organizations, policies, and initiatives targeting Black school children was centered on the largely unproven and anti-Black theories, practices, and values of White people. In isolation, I read, studied, and practiced the ideas from this rich repository on Black education. Yet, those works were rarely if ever on the syllabi for my courses. Black scholars and practitioners were not invited for professional development in the districts in which I worked, and the classroom practices inspired by their work were neither recognized, encouraged, nor funded. At the ABEN Institutes, however, not just one but nearly all these works, practitioners, educational, scholars and theorists were engaged with educators from across the nation. I found it to be a radical, transformative resistance to White domination in education. This radicality, transformation, and resistance was further operationalized through the networking among the participants. Through their Institutes, ABEN was creating an undercurrent in the ocean that is the tyranny of Whiteness in Black education. The various ABEN youth programs I witnessed from afar were, too. I can only imagine how far along we'd be if these programs were adopted by public schools across this nation.

In 2018, I attended the regional ABEN institute in Philadelphia where I met Debra Watkins in person for the first time. I latched onto her immediately, told her about my work with Sisters In Education Circle (SIEC), and insisted that she'd become one of my jegnas. By this time in my career, I had launched two organizations and it became clear the Ancestors were calling me to become an institution builder like Debra Watkins. With the love, encouragement, and thought partnership of personal sister elders in education, I created the SIEC community to put current and potential Black women educators in intimate relationship with pioneering Black women educators and the ancestors that influence their work. In mainstream educational spaces, these connections are intentionally severed. Yet, it's these connections that enable me to do my soul work, inspiring the natural genius of Black young people despite the imperatives of the White power structure. The forces of anti-Blackness in public school systems consistently misdirect time, attention, and resources away from the natural genius of Black children and the pedagogical genius of Black educators. Throughout my entire career, I've been able to call up two of my anchors, Lisa Delpit and Linda Mizell; turn to the work of one of my lighthouses—Vanessa Siddle Walker, Theresa Perry, Michele Foster, bell hooks, Gloria Ladson-Billings, and many more; or lean into the legacy of our North stars including Mary McLeod Bethune, Harriet Tubman, Septima Clark, and many more. These torches always gave me more knowledge, clarity, and strength for the journey, like a clean glass of water. I built SIEC to share these experiences with other Black women educators. I have been blessed with a loving circle of jegnas who have contributed to Black education in many powerful ways; however, it became clear to me that having a jegna who has also been called to institution building would be crucial. Debra was cordial and encouraging. She even gave me her cell phone number. Yet, we would not connect again until I reached out a couple years later to ask her to be a sister elder in education at the 2021 SIEC retreat and during the 2020 – 2021 monthly virtual gatherings. After we spoke a few times, I noticed she began to ask me questions about my organization. Did I have an executive summary? A budget? Who was funding my work? These questions quickly turned into her guiding me in developing all these aspects of my organization and eventually led me to receiving my first large grant. This grant allowed me to hire myself and continue to build SIEC. I learned that there are many organizations, projects, and individuals that Mama Debra has supported in this way. This, too, is part of the radical nature of Debra Watkins and ABEN's work, beginning with the Institutes and flowing out exponentially from them.

Throughout my schooling and career, I independently explored a rich body of work on Black teaching excellence that is nearly six generations deep. ABEN foregrounds many of these thinkers in its work. This exploration was augmented by the stories of excellent Black teachers I grew up hearing about from elders within my community. When I became a teacher, I noticed I had a particular orientation toward teaching and Black children. These were impulses I shared with several other Black teachers but were clearly distinct from most of my White colleagues. In my dissertation, I completed a literature review of these works. These works were highly descriptive; many of them were rich historical accounts, and a few of them identified key characteristics of Black teaching excellence. I combed through this literature looking for specific pedagogical elements. My review yielded nine elements that I termed the "Black teaching tradition" (BTT). ABEN is an embodiment of all nine elements and most especially *believing*.

> Believing: Black teachers approach instruction from the unwavering standpoint that Black culture(s) are rich and positive, and with the conviction that Black students have limitless intellectual capacity and potential for success. In alignment with the community member/extended family role, Black teachers hold a collectively positive view of Black culture(s), themselves, and their students as community members. (Lesesne, 2020, p. 45)

My mother and sister still live in the house where we grew up. It's in Parkway, my neighborhood in South Florida. My first memories of Black girl magic and Black boy joy were made there. My childhood home was like a nest built on a low branch, full of care but not far enough out of the way of harm from outside elements. Just outside this nest were the vicissitudes of anti-Blackness engrained in the very fabric of this country at its inception and ready to consume Black children like my siblings, my childhood friends, and me. After desegregation, school buildings would become White-led and White-dominated sites of terror for Black children and Black educators. For as long as this terror has existed, there has been a tradition of Black resistance to the tyranny of Whiteness in Black education. Debra Watkins and ABEN sit squarely in that tradition, and she is ensuring that tradition continues through support of a wide array of projects, individuals' work, and organizations. I'm thankful that my work is included in these efforts.

Questions

What are the anti-Black spaces that you navigate on a daily basis? Identify your lighthouses and healing practices for preserving your soul.

References

Delpit, L. D. (2006). *Other people's children: Cultural conflict in the classroom*. New Press.

Lesesne, P. (2020). "A sistah circle of seven: Black women's self-perceptions of their Teach for America (TFA) experiences in the U.S. Mid-Atlantic region" (2020). *Dissertation available from ProQuest*. AAI28157533.

View, J. L., Frank, T. J., & Williams, A. (2019, Nov. 14–17). *Conversations across the decades: Learning African American pedagogical excellence from Black mathematical "dreamkeepers"* [Paper presentation]. North American Chapter of the International Group for the Psychology of Mathematics Education.

TEN

Full Circle: A Tribute to Debra Watkins and ABEN

Bobbie Brooks

Debra Watkins is a very giving spirit and a powerful warrior for those who comprise our African American village. If you are willing to commit time and energy to nurture and build our village, then you will find a kindred spirit in her.

I met Debra in 2003. I had recently been promoted to the Assistant Superintendent of Educational Services for the Alameda County Office of Education (ACOE) located in Hayward, California. Our meeting proved serendipitous. During my tenure as the Assistant Superintendent for Educational Services, the mandate from the California State Department of Education for County Offices of Education (COE) was to raise the achievement level for historically underperforming students. My department was responsible for providing professional development opportunities to the 18 school districts within Alameda County.

A critical component for successful implementation of this initiative was attending meetings every six weeks in Sacramento to receive requisite training and materials and review current disaggregated student performance data. It was disheartening to see that no matter how the data was presented, African American students scored at the very bottom. At that time, I was the only County Office of Education Assistant Superintendent for Educational Services in the state of California who was African American. Not only was I infuriated by the scores, but also by the matter-of-fact acceptance displayed by most of my colleagues in the room. Sadly, after many years as an educator holding school district positions of special education teacher, educational diagnostician (pre-school – high school), elementary school principal, and grade level director of elementary education, adding this statewide perspective forced me to face the horrific reality that many in positions of power and/or authority in education held as their truth - ***School failure and African American children is as ice cream is to cake; they just go together.***

When schools and districts engage in this kind of institutionalized racist thinking, the failure of African American students becomes a self-fulfilling prophecy of lower expectations. I noticed that within these school site settings, a sense of urgency to fully address why most of their African American students consistently underperform academically was not meaningfully addressed, even in districts with highly qualified teachers and well-resourced schools. Staff is often hesitant to and/or avoids using research-based teaching materials and classroom teacher strategies proven successful in raising the academic performance of African American students. An equally disturbing pattern of behavior is the practiced excuses given as to why they were not able to provide sufficient resources to accelerate the students' academic growth. Within the confines of educational institutions that exhibit such inherent biases, typically if the concern addresses the academic issue for African American students, their solution to solving the problems is to blame the African American students and their parents as opposed to accepting their responsibility and working in partnership with the students, families, and the African American school community to improve student outcomes. Painfully, their lack of concern manifests itself in low student performance for African American students, generation after generation.

The convergence of my professional observations and personal outrage led me to intensify my efforts to change this paradigm. After devoting countless hours to researching scenarios documenting African American students succeeding, I concluded that grass-roots, community-based support programs yielded the most effective results. I reached out to the African American educators and community advocates in Southern Alameda County to share this idea. I quickly garnered support and was able to recruit four volunteers to serve as board members to establish an African American educators' community-based organization. After several board meetings, we recognized that if our organization were to flourish, we needed a creative jegna and advocate to work with, who was savvy in designing highly effective educational programs and services that would enable African American children and their families to achieve beyond the low expectations the system set for them. Preferably, the programs would have the flexibility to operate successfully outside of the restrictions and tensions of the educational institution.

We also agreed that our fledgling organization needed to affiliate with a state or national organization for support. An online search revealed that an organization called the California Alliance of African American Educators

(CAAAE), was having a Professional Development Breakfast the following weekend. The Breakfast was being held at the Westin Hotel in Santa Clara, CA—just a 25-mile drive. We were overjoyed! I contacted the name listed on the website, Founder and President, Ms. Debra Watkins, to ask if our team could register late. By the end of the rich and culturally relevant professional development event, we realized we had found a home! She embodied each criterion we sought. We paid the small affiliation fee shortly thereafter and became CAAAE's first affiliate as the Southern Alameda County Alliance of African American Educators (SACAAAE). I didn't have any idea of the extraordinary impact meeting Debra Watkins that day would have on the future of my career.

My vision as an educator has always been to teach, uplift and support African American students and their families. Debra Watkins enabled me to accomplish my vision by providing hands-on training and support in establishing SACAAAE and execution of my responsibilities as the CAAAE San Francisco Bay Area Regional Co-Coordinator.

Southern Alameda County Alliance of African American Educators (SACAAAE)

As an affiliate, we modeled the mission and events of CAAAE, with modifications as necessary, to meet the specific needs of our Southern Alameda County student and family community. I informed Debra Watkins that I was very inexperienced in how to start and operate a nonprofit organization. She informed me that SACAAAE would need to obtain a 501(c)(3) status before we could accept donations to support our programs and services and connected me with the CAAAE treasurer for assistance. Given that I was president and founder of SACAAAE, she advised me to attend the excellent Compass Point leadership workshops for nonprofits to acquire the skills necessary to build a successful organization. For me, one of the key takeaways from the workshop was that nonprofits tend to evolve over time.

I shared with Debra Watkins the three reasons that compelled me to start the community-based organization in Southern Alameda County, with blatant racism being the driving force. First, I wanted to change the tendency to primarily reference African American students and their families, whether in academics or behavior, as part of a deficit model. I wanted to have a Southern countywide event that highlighted African American students achieving at high levels in various areas that evidenced the level of their parents' engagement. Secondly, I wanted to decrease the sense of isolation experienced by African American educators. Often, there were only one or two on staff and, at other times, there were none. My goal was to host a gathering where they could come together in a safe environment and just exhale. My third driving force was to increase the visibility of African Americans in Southern Alameda County. This area of the county borders East Oakland. For whatever reason, the prevailing assumption at that time was that once you left Oakland, African Americans ceased to exist! Having worked in Oakland Unified for 20 years prior, I was knowledgeable about programs and services that African American students could be eligible for if the providers were aware of their existence and needs.

Debra Watkins responded, "I have the perfect event for you." She described the cultural pursuits student achievement awards in detail to me. I shared that I was both elated and felt a little overwhelmed at the same time. She commented with authority, "You can do it" and immediately verbalized a plan of action. She began preparing me to have a successful event almost immediately. True to her word, she invited me to the Santa Clara County Alliance of Black Educators' Cultural Pursuits Student Achievement Awards in 2003 and 2004. They honored 250 students in transitional grades 5th, 8th, and 12th in six different categories. She spoke with the president of the organization (Debra Watkins was also a member) and asked him if he would forward their award materials and planning list to me.

Cultural Pursuits Student Achievement Awards

SACAAAE held its first Cultural Pursuits Student Achievement Awards ceremony in 2005. Our theme was "Creating a College-Going Culture." We honored 23 proud students during our first year, with 125 elated family, friends, and educators in attendance in the boardroom at the Alameda County Office of Education in Hayward, CA. We were happily surprised to see parents carrying flowers and balloons as they entered the room. It confirmed for us that we were on the right track in fulfilling the silent cry for recognition after years of neglect regarding our youth and their families, who were doing good things.

We were eternally grateful for Debra Watkins' presence at that first award event. The constructive criticism she offered regarding how to increase district and student participation, and best practices for me to engage SACAAAE's board members during the event, proved invaluable beyond measure. Most importantly was her directive for me to go to the top and meet with each of the 10 district superintendents in Southern Alameda County. When I tried to push back and meet only with my peer group, she explained that you need to meet with the superintendents directly because they are the decision makers. Her sage advice enabled our awards event to grow exponentially from 23 to 350 honorees in attendance (550 had been selected) and a capacity crowd of 1,182 within four years at the Chabot College of Performing Arts. After nine years, I sunset SACAAAE for personal reasons and helped create a new organization called the African American Regional Educational Alliances to continue our impactful work. To date, we have honored 4,250 proud, young, gifted, and Black students and their families! Pre-COVID-19, it was always exciting to see superintendents, teachers and counselors posing and taking pictures with students from their district. Chabot always provides a wonderful reception for the event and there's an impressive live band playing on the platform until the reception ends. It is a magical day from beginning to end. In 2022, we hosted our 18th Student Achievement Awards ceremony. For the 3rd year, due to COVID-19, it was a zoom event.

The Awards ceremony has become a signature event in Southern Alameda County. It has had a far reaching influence on the Southern Alameda County educational community and beyond! An unexpected but powerful outcome was the trusting relationship that emerged between the districts and SACAAAE. This provided an opportunity for us to meet annually with district superintendents. We were able to obtain their permission to meet with and provide presentations during district-level principal meetings, school-site staff meetings, and parent groups on creating a college-going culture for their African American student population. We introduced concepts of culturally relevant instructional practices during the presentations as the best practice to apply to successfully achieve this goal.

In addition, the Awards event helped us establish strong partnerships with most of the entities we needed to apply for a 4-year state grant that resulted in the creation of the Southern Alameda County Regional Education Alliances (SACREA). Furthermore, at least two of the partners were able to acquire grants for their individual organizations because of their working relationship with the SACAAAE.

SACAAAE's Back to School Reception for African American Educators

This event was a phenomenal, uplifting experience for the African American staff working in isolation. It was held in a Black-owned venue to create a culturally nurturing and supportive environment. The educators appreciated the opportunity to gather in a space that felt safe and welcoming. They embraced the moment with great enthusiasm. It was exciting to witness their joy in coming together as a community and interacting with peers from other districts or just connecting with old friends in a relaxed environment. The event fulfilled the important basic human needs of being seen and heard.

Evolution to AAREA

AAREA evolved over time. In 2012, the Southern Alameda County Alliance of African American Educators (SACAAAE), an affiliate of CAAAE; the Choose College Educational Foundation, an affiliate of R.T. Fisher Educational Enterprises (RTF); and the Southern Alameda County Regional Educational Alliances (SACREA), joined forces to form the African American Regional Education Alliances, (AAREA). AAREA is the culmination of almost 10 years of work to support educational achievement among African American students. The "call to action" for forming the alliance was the realization that, although the three organizations had made enormous contributions to Southern Alameda County's African American community, a review of data revealed a collective need to extend our services throughout Alameda County and into the greater San Francisco Bay Area and beyond.

AAAREA initiatives include: African American Student Achievement and Excellence Awards (formerly the Cultural Pursuits Student Achievement Awards, modified and renamed in 2012); Professional Development Summit (formerly the Professional Development Breakfast, expanded and renamed in 2012); STEM S.T.E.P.S. for success; back-to-school reception for African American educators; Pastors' leadership breakfast; Regional Parent Network Initiative.

Debra Watkins believes in reaching out to support those who are working to help prepare African American children for success. She was our guiding force for SACAAAE. Even though SACAAAE no longer exists, she continues to support AAREA by advertising the events in her newsletter and website;

she has donated funds for one of the initiatives and readily shares information with her networks.

California Alliance of African American Educators (CAAAE)

I had the opportunity to attend conferences and training hosted by very reputable institutions of higher learning or by professional educational leadership organizations held in high regard. The speakers were presented as being the best and brightest experts in their fields. Admittedly, I learned valuable information that I was able to successfully apply in whatever position I held at that time. But after receiving training from some the best national and international African American researchers (Drs. Geneva Gay, Carol Lee, Pedro Noguera, Joyce King, Gloria Ladson-Billings, Noma LeMoine, Sharokky Hollie, just to name a few), I realized that the ABEN Institute was different. Instead of exiting the Institute feeling exhausted or that my issues were overlooked or sometimes attacked, as was my typical demeanor, I felt rejuvenated and excited about what I had learned and the creative ways I could employ it as a change agent. I realized that my response was different because Debra Watkins structured the Institute with deep purpose and thought.

She limited the number of participants, which created a more intimate setting and significantly increased opportunities for learning. As participants, we were close enough to make direct eye contact with the speakers. It felt as if they were having a conversation with us as opposed to the lecture or standard presentation. The method she used to facilitate the full group activities prevented the typical demeaning pushbacks, vicious verbal combativeness, and someone monopolizing the conversation. As a result, you felt safe to ask a question and that your voice mattered. The tone for the Institute had been set by the time the breakout groups occurred. The presentation of the food was always beautiful as well as delicious! My spiritual roots were soothed and culturally well-fed every year that I attended the institute.

I was excited and grateful that in my role as assistant superintendent, I could directly engage the appropriate district staff person(s) to send teams to the Institute and receive the powerful training on culturally relevant pedagogy from African American PhDs. I had the pleasure of personally witnessing how it helped create the beginning of a cultural shift in three districts with which my staff and I worked very closely. The superintendent from one of those districts brought her entire staff of 25 administrators to the Institute.

Professional Development Breakfasts (PDB)

As the CAAAE co-coordinator for the Bay Area, my committee and I were responsible for hosting a breakfast for our area. Because I was new to the role and didn't know any of the other members very well, Debra Watkins graciously selected the members for me. She also provided each of the 10 regional co-coordinators with $500 to cover the basic expenses to host their breakfasts. I was impressed to discover that Debra Watkins raised the $5000 needed all by herself. I quickly learned to select one of the presenters from the ABEN Summer Institute as the speaker for the Bay Area PDB. The benefits were two-fold. It enabled those who were not able to attend the Institute to receive the information/training and afforded the opportunity to consider contracting with the presenter to train their staff in culturally relevant instructional practices. Over a 3-year period, Dr. Darlene Willis, Dr. Noma Lemoine, and Dr. Edwin Javius were each invited to present at one of our PDBs. They each did a fabulous job and were sought after by several districts after their presentations. Black Educators were also honored with awards for excellence for their commitment and extraordinary work during this event.

CAAAE to A Black Education Network

I worked very closely with Debra Watkins when she was founder, president, and executive director of CAAAE. It was clear that her worth had grown beyond California. She had begun to connect with people from across the country who were equally impressed with her work. She and I had several conversations about her stepping into the national arena, and others who had planted that seed years ago were still encouraging her to move up to the next level. Just as she encouraged me when I decided to merge SACAAAE with AAREA so that I could enjoy my retirement, I wanted to support her. I attended the initial planning meetings for ABEN in Atlanta and the ABEN conference in Chicago. Both events were powerfully steeped in the culture of the motherland. I never cease to be amazed at Debra Watkins' ability to bring together great African American minds to provide training to accelerate and create access to learning opportunities for our students. I was riveted by the keynote speakers and workshop leaders, but I was completely mesmerized by the Kinsey Collection presentation. After 9 years of working closely with her, I came to expect nothing less from my friend, Debra Watkins.

Reflections

The African proverbs, "If your vision is for a year, plant wheat; if your vision is for a decade, plant trees; and if your vision is for a lifetime, plant people" and "With a little seed of imagination, you can grow a field of hope," aptly describe the impact and sustainability for the legacy of Debra Watkins' body of work.

Debra Watkins captures the imagination of people and plants seeds of confidence and hope within them. I was one of the many individuals who was a direct beneficiary of her bountiful determination and humanitarianism. In the field of education, we often hear the phrase "closing the achievement gap" or "closing the opportunity gap" in reference to student learning. However, what we do not often hear about is an educator voluntarily working to "close the funding and opportunity gap" for small underfunded African American community-based organizations and/or individual advocates struggling daily to meet the educational needs of the students and families in their respective communities. Debra Watkins is such a person.

She is a prolific writer and has used her gift to acquire resources and grant funding to help support these efforts. During my tenure as president of SACAAAE and co-coordinator and member of the CAAAE Executive Board, most important to me was observing her mastery for designing structures that created opportunities for those she worked with to build the capacity to grow/evolve and sustain their organizations, if they chose to do so. She was very hands-on and worked just as hard as all the volunteers she recruited to serve in various positions to ensure that everyone's events were a success. For Debra Watkins, failing our community was just not an option. This was one of the many values that she and I have in common. I continue to be in awe of how she regularly traveled between Northern and Southern California to be physically present to support various events while still working as a high school teacher, and she has yet to slow down. She continues to juggle three or four major challenging efforts at once and each one always yields extraordinary results.

I appreciated every opportunity that she provided for me to grow, to learn, and to continually be culturally and spiritually fed. Debra Watkins has been a wonderful thought partner, jegna, friend, and advocate. I appreciate everything that she has unselfishly done for our African American community on a local, state, and national level, and the love, support, and thoughtfulness she has consistently shown toward my family. She is an indomitable warrior and a living legend.

Questions

Hold a mirror to your practice. What is your 360? How do you think people will talk about your work in retrospect?

AFTERWORD

What Traditional Teacher Education Can Learn From A Black Education Network

Marvin Lynn, PhD

A Black Education Network (ABEN), with its insistence on using soul-centered approaches to advancing the academic achievement of Black students, could be instrumental in the possible transformation of teacher education in significant ways. I am a lifelong teacher educator. For the last 25 years, I have worked either as an adjunct faculty member, a tenure-track and tenured faculty member, a program coordinator, an associate dean, or a dean with deep engagement in teacher education in primarily public institutions serving urban areas. I spent about 15 years teaching in these programs. For the last decade, I've worked as a full-time administrator overseeing these programs. I have also been engaged in examining the links between race, education, teacher diversity, and success of Black students, particularly males, in the context of urban K-12 classrooms. As someone who has directly engaged with teacher education programs in predominantly White institutions for 2 decades while also pursuing an active research agenda with an explicit focus on race and racism, I have often been disillusioned by the extent to which teacher education programs have failed to address issues impacting Black students. I've written about this in *Diverse Issues in Higher Education* (Lynn, 2014, 2020).

Teacher education programs are shaped and influenced by practitioners and scholars who may lack exposure to environments where there are a diverse set of perspectives and experiences. In other words, "We can't teach what we don't know" (Howard, 1999). Howard wrote about the knowledge problem facing mostly White preschool–12 teachers in the United States and argued that this was a significant barrier to their ability to effectively teach an increasingly diverse student body. While I agree that teacher education faces a similar challenge because higher education faculty are also overwhelmingly

White, I also believe that our challenge is far more complex. As folks with doctorates, we make active choices about the forms of knowledge we deem legitimate and worthy. In the field of education, race and culture has always been undertheorized and ignored. Scholars of race, culture, and language in the field have fought to change this over the last several decades. It is not within the scope of this afterword to offer an extensive overview of the rich tapestry of scholarship in these areas. However, these scholars, many of them recognized by the most prestigious research and teaching organizations in the world, are still fighting for legitimacy and trying to convince the field that this knowledge is worthy and essential for the preparation of teachers of diverse learners. Despite the decades of work in this area, the curriculum in teacher preparation programs is designed to prepare teachers to teach White, monolingual, heterosexual, cisgender, middle-class male children. As a result, teacher candidates are simply not well-prepared to effectively teach Black children.

The challenges facing teacher preparation are not solely related to curriculum or the complexion of the faculty. Teacher education programs are embedded within a complex web of social, political, and economic formations that limit and restrict opportunities for these programs to expand beyond their current boundaries. For example, in most states, licensure standards are extremely limited and require programs to teach specific courses in what are considered the fundamental content areas. Elementary education curriculum typically focuses on reading, math, and social studies with an increasingly limited focus on science. In some cases, the content in those courses is also laid out. For example, a certain number of reading courses is required for elementary teachers. In some states, faculty are also required to teach "the science of reading" and address issues such as "dyslexia." These restrictions create challenges for professors who may be interested, for example, in helping teacher-education candidates understand the important links between literacy, language, and culture. Middle- and high school content focuses almost entirely on content with a limited focus on pedagogy and typically almost no room for discussion about interdisciplinary teaching or the values of Africana studies. Extensive and heavily prescribed state requirements for teachers also make it challenging for faculty members to add additional content requirements to the curriculum without increasing students' time to degree. As a dean in Oregon, I had conversations with the state director of teacher licensure to ask him to consider giving teacher education programs more freedom to experiment with different types of curricula. There was reluctance to create greater flexibility in the licensure standards because of testing requirements for teachers seeking licensure. Rigid curricular demands are tied to tests that are tied to the general public's emphasis on what they would define as rigor. This is enforced by the legislature.

The challenges facing teacher education are complex because, although staffing, state licensure standards, and curriculum play a key role in the inadequate preparation of teachers for teaching historically underserved populations, a teacher's readiness to teach diverse learners is also related to that candidate's worldview, their prior knowledge, experiences, and their readiness to shift their own biases in order to form close relationships with students whose culture, race, ethnicity, and language they may not share. There are numerous research articles written by faculty of color who have received harsh reviews from White students who did not appreciate their efforts to push their thinking on issues of race. Teacher education students have agency. They often utilize that agency to ensure that the curriculum is focused mainly on issues they deem relevant and important. They also use their power to limit professional advancement opportunities for faculty members who consistently challenge them to critically self-reflect and think differently about their students and the communities they serve. My own experience of "learning to teach" provides a counternarrative that illuminates the power of personal experience and what it means to teach to the soul.

I started my career as an elementary school teacher in the early 1990s. I was dismayed by the way Black children were treated in these school settings, both public and private. As a young teacher, I experienced remarkable success with my Black students. Attendance rates improved. Grades and test scores improved. Some of my students went on to have great careers and publicly acknowledge the influence I had on their academic preparation.

My preparation for teaching started with a deep immersion in my own community and other Black communities in Chicago. First of all, I was born and raised in the Englewood community, historically one of Chicago's poorest and most hypersegregated Black communities on the Southside of Chicago. I had deep personal experience and connection to this community and sought, through my professional experiences, to gain exposure to other communities that were similar in nature. As a result, I tutored and taught part-time in elementary schools in what was formerly known as The Cabrini-Green Projects, Uptown, and the Englewood neighborhoods of Chicago well before I entered a teacher education program. I entered the teacher education program as a Golden Apple Scholar of Illinois. Through the Golden Apple Scholars program, I continued to be engaged in schools in the summer. I worked in a school that served what was called the Robert Taylor Homes. The Robert Taylor Homes were a notorious housing project on the Southside of Chicago that served thousands of mostly poor African American children. I can recall working under the tutelage of a well-liked White educator who had a reputation for having a Black cultural style. He did not hold the students to high expectations, however.

There were other experiences, both personal and professional, that helped ground me as a teacher. On an intellectual level, I took courses on Black history, race, class, gender, and critical pedagogy. By the time I student taught, I was reasonably well-situated with the knowledge of Black history and culture and had been introduced to Paulo Freire's work as well as the work of Black scholars who were writing in the culturally responsive education tradition. At the same time, I was being mentored by Dr. Sandra Jackson and Dr. Vera Rhimes, Black women professors who practiced the "racial uplift" tradition and worked hard to ensure that Black students were successful. I also had deep roots in the Black community of Englewood in Chicago's Southside and grew up with a mother from the Delta region of Mississippi, birthplace of the blues. As a result, I'm steeped in our community's cultural traditions, and I possess an intimate knowledge of our history and culture. In that sense, I had a number of conditions in my personal and professional life that set me up for success as an educator of Black children. My teacher education program provided me with a credential but ultimately did not prepare me to successfully teach Black children. My great Black professors taught courses on culture, race, and philosophy of education. They did not teach the methods courses. Those courses were reserved for White faculty who had little to no knowledge about how to teach math, science, reading, or social studies to Black children. I drew on my own knowledge of Black history and culture to enhance the curriculum and my teaching practice.

Unfortunately, teachers are still being prepared to teach in the same way that I was taught. They take methods courses that are disconnected from broader issues of race, culture, class, and gender. If they are fortunate, they take one or more courses that deal with issues of race and culture as philosophical, social, and political issues. They are not taught to think about how the curriculum is racialized. They certainly are not taking courses in Black history and culture.

Teacher education must change if it is going to remain relevant. Dr. Rona Frederick and Dr. Kmt Shockley, through their investigation of the work of Debra Watkins, provide a possible pathway for that transformation to occur. For many decades, Joyce King, her jegna, has been at the vanguard of the Black education movement. Debra Watkins has worked alongside Dr. King to ensure that Black educators had the necessary moral support to advance their teaching on behalf of Black students. Both Joyce King and Debra Watkins have put forward a vision for Black education that is African-centered, holistic, community-grounded, intellectually rigorous, and intentionally humanistic—soul-centered. It is grounded in theory but also practical in nature. I would argue that this provides an excellent framework for the ways in which we ought to be thinking about teacher education today. Joyce King in her recent testimony to the California Legislature makes this point in incredible detail. LaGarrett King's research also clarifies the benefits associated with situating the preparation of teachers within the Black Studies tradition. In fact, his work clarifies for me that providing student teachers with deep knowledge and expertise in Black history can positively shape not only their outlook but their ability to effectively teach Black children and other children of color.

At Portland State University, where I served as dean of the College of Education, I proposed the York Institute for the Study of Race and Education. The Institute serves as a space where Ethnic Studies faculty can work closely with education faculty to:

- strengthen and enhance the teacher education curriculum to better incorporate aspects of ethnic studies (particularly Black studies);
- provide a space where ethnic studies faculty can collaborate with educational faculty to provide in-service teachers with needed professional development on how to teach the new ethnic studies standards required in Oregon beginning in 2025.

In addition, there have been discussions about the need to situate teacher education more squarely within Black studies. The State of Oregon has made it possible for nontraditional programs to be granted the opportunity to partner with a variety of community agencies to advance teacher preparation on behalf of communities of color. There would be the opportunity for the Black Studies program at Portland State University to partner with a variety of Black-led community-based organizations to develop their own teacher education program that would situate the preparation of Black teachers and others within Black history and culture. As I write this, I am preparing to move to another institution to take a deanship. I hope to remain connected to Portland State as a consultant in order to see this effort through. I also hope to foster the same types of relationships in Denver.

I've outlined a number of challenges facing our field. One other challenge is the degree of isolation and the lack of connection that universities sometimes experience. While community engagement is often touted as a universal value in most institutions of higher education, they often practice policies of self-interest that actually harm communities of color. ABEN could provide support to institutions of higher education regarding the best practices for strengthening relationships with local Black communities and supporting schools in the effort to advance Black student achievement at all levels. The advancement of Black student achievement will necessarily impact the retention and success of Black students in higher education where there are also challenges with Black student success. At the end of the day, this kind of relationship actually serves institutions of higher education well. As I move forward to another institutional context, I look forward to working closely with ABEN and similar organizations to form partnerships to advance Black achievement.

References

Howard, G. R. (1999). *We can't teach what we don't know: White teachers, multiracial schools.* Teachers College Press.

Lynn, M. (2014, Mar. 19). Making culturally relevant pedagogy relevant to aspiring teachers. *Diverse Issues in Higher Education.* Matthew Cox & Associates.

Lynn, M. (2020, Dec. 31). Reflecting back to move equity in education forward. *Diverse Issues in Higher Education.* Matthew Cox & Associates.

About the Authors

Bobbie Brooks received a Bachelor of Science degree from the University of California, Berkeley and a Masters in Special Education from Saint Mary's College in Moraga, CA. An educator for over 30 years, she served as an assistant superintendent of Educational Services, Elementary Grade-Level director, principal, and special educator. She was also an adjunct professor in the Principals Leadership Institute at University of California, Berkeley. Ms. Brooks has received numerous awards in recognition of her work.

Anthony T. Browder is an author, cultural historian, and educational consultant. He is a graduate of Howard University and has lectured extensively throughout the United States and five continents. Mr. Browder is director of IKG Cultural Resources and has devoted 44 years to researching ancient Egyptian history and culture. He is currently director of the ASA Restoration Project, which is funding the excavation of 25th-Dynasty tombs in Luxor, Egypt. Browder is also cofounder and codirector of the Cultural Imperative Initiative.

Rona M. Frederick, PhD serves as a coordinator of Education Studies at the Catholic University of America. She has written more than a dozen research articles on culturally responsive teaching of children of African ancestry. She holds a Bachelor's Degree in Psychology from Hampton University, a Master's Degree in Professional Studies with a focus on Africana studies from Cornell University, and a Doctoral Degree in Curriculum and Instruction with a focus on teacher education, evaluation, and equity from the University of Maryland, College Park.

Joyce E. King (BA, PhD Stanford University) is the Benjamin Mays endowed chair for Urban Teaching, Learning and Leadership and Professor of Educational Policy Studies at Georgia State University. A past president of the American Educational Research Association, she was provost at Spelman College and director of teacher education at Santa Clara. Her recent books include *Heritage knowledge in the curriculum* (with E. Swartz) and *We be lovin'*

Black children: Learning to be literate about the African diaspora (co-editors G. Boutte, G. Jackson, & L. King).

Rev. Akosua Lesesne, EdD is an educational design leader and creator of a teacher development framework for Black pedagogical genius that she termed the Black Teaching Tradition (BTT). She is the founder of Sisters in Education Circle (SIEC) and Lesesne Legacy Learning Village (Lesesne Learning). She earned a Bachelor's Degree from Harvard University, a Master of Arts in Teaching from Tufts University, and a Doctorate in Educational and Organizational Leadership at the University of Pennsylvania Graduate School of Education.

Marvin Lynn, PhD is professor and dean in the School of Education and Human Development at the University of Colorado, Denver. He is one of the leading scholars in the field of race and education and is quoted regularly in local, national, and international news stories. He is the lead editor of *The handbook of critical race theory in education*, which is in its second edition.

Ayinde Olokotin is a proud alumnus of the Greene Scholars Program, which has profoundly impacted his academic and personal growth. He is presently a junior at Pomona College, majoring in Philosophy, Politics, and Economics, a Pomona College Judicial Board member, and a proud proponent of programs like GSP that help Black children realize their full academic potential. With a background in community organization, his political consulting and policy research work focuses on his community's greater enfranchisement and social advancement.

Kmt Shockley, PhD is professor of educational leadership at the University of Houston. His interests include research on African-centered education and maroonage.

Monica Z. Utsey-Okpoti is an educator, writer, HIM Tours Ghana travel Coordinator, digital content creator and 20+ year homeschool veteran. In 2004, she co-founded the Sankofa Homeschool Community, a support group for homeschoolers of the African Diaspora. In 2011, she led the expansion of the Sankofa Homeschool Community with the founding of the Sankofa

Homeschool Collective. Currently, she works as a reading tutor for the Maya Angelou Young Adult Learning Center.

Debra Watkins graduated from Pitzer College in 1976 with a BA in English with minors in French and psychology. In 1977, Debra earned a Masters in Education and lifetime teaching credentials in English, French, and psychology from Stanford University. She taught high school English and served as a counselor and project coordinator for 37 years. Debra is the founder and executive director of A Black Education Network, the Dr. Frank S. Greene Scholars STEM Program, and cofounder of Black Students of California United.

Index